ALSO BY GEORGE McGOVERN

The Essential America

The Third Freedom: Ending Hunger in Our Time

Terry: My Daughter's Life-and-Death Struggle with Alcoholism

War Against Want

Grassroots: The Autobiography of George S. McGovern

The Great Coalfield War (with Leonard Guttridge)

An American Journey:
The Presidential Campaign Speeches of George McGovern

A Time of War, a Time of Peace

Agricultural Thought in the Twentieth Century

ALSO BY WILLIAM R. POLK

The Birth of America

Understanding Iraq

Polk's Folly: An American Family History

Passing Brave

The Opening of South Lebanon 1788–1840:
A Study of the Impact of the West on the Middle East

Neighbors and Strangers: The Fundamentals of Foreign Affairs

The Golden Ode (translator)

The Elusive Peace: The Middle East in the Twentieth Century

The United States and the Arab World

The Arab World Today

OUT OF

IRAQ

A PRACTICAL PLAN FOR WITHDRAWAL NOW

George S. McGovern
and William R. Polk

SIMON & SCHUSTER PAPERBACKS
NEW YORK   LONDON   TORONTO   SYDNEY

SIMON & SCHUSTER PAPERBACKS
Rockefeller Center
1230 Avenue of the Americas
New York, NY 10020

Designed by Joel Avirom/Jason Snyder

For information regarding special discounts for bulk purchases,
please contact Simon & Schuster Special Sales at
1-800-456-6798 or business@simonandschuster.com

Manufactured in the United States of America

3   5   7   9   10   8   6   4

Library of Congress Cataloging-in-Publication Data is available.

ISBN-13: 978-1-4165-3456-3
ISBN-10: 1-4165-3456-3

This book is dedicated to our grandchildren, with the hope that they will profit from the lessons we should have learned in Iraq, and to the Americans and Iraqis who have lost their lives in this disastrous war.

The provision of the Constitution giving the war-making power to Congress was dictated, as I understand it, by the following reasons. Kings had always been involving and impoverishing their people in wars, pretending generally, if not always, that the good of the people was the object. This, our [Constitutional] Convention understood to be the most oppressive of all Kingly oppressions; and they resolved to so frame the Constitution that no one man should hold the power of bringing this oppression upon us.

—Letter to William Herndon
on February 15, 1848, from Abraham Lincoln

CONTENTS

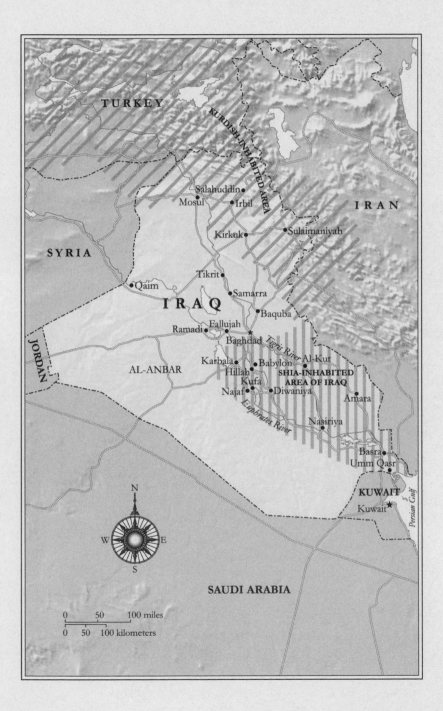

FOREWORD

Why We Wrote This Book

EVENTS HAVE PROVEN that the U.S. government's decision to invade and occupy Iraq in 2003 was a calamitous mistake. So far more than 2,500 young Americans have been killed; more than 16,000 have been wounded, half of them with disabilities that can never be repaired; and more than 40,000 have received severe psychological damage for which they, and we, will be paying for decades to come. As bad as these results of the war have been, they are just the beginning. The Defense and Veterans Brain Injury Center has learned that perhaps one in every ten—about 50,000—returning soldiers has suffered a concussion whose effects—memory loss, severe headaches, and confused thinking—will linger throughout his or her life. Exposure to depleted uranium is expected to add thousands of more patients, many of whom will develop cancer, to hospitals run by the Department of Veterans Affairs.

No one knows how many Iraqi civilians the United States has killed. Estimates run from 30,000 to 100,000. Since Iraq has a total population of less than 10 percent of America's, even the lowest estimate means that virtually every Iraqi has a relative, neighbor, or friend whose death he or she blames on us. A whole society has been crippled and may not recover for a generation or more. President George W. Bush and his team originally told us that we invaded Iraq in search of weapons of mass destruction that were an "imminent threat" to the United States. When no such weapons were found, we were told that our army had invaded Iraq to bring democracy. Military force may change a regime, but it cannot create democracy.

President Bush and his team have also told us—are still telling us—that they sent and want to keep our army in Iraq to destroy terrorism. But as we now know—and as they knew then—Iraq had nothing to do with the 9/11 terrorist attacks on America. Our war against Iraq is not reducing terrorism or making us safe. Rather, it is breeding terrorists in large and increasing numbers and giving them a base of operations among people who now hate our country. The longer we occupy Iraq, the greater will be the danger to America.

The material costs of the war will likely almost bankrupt our economy. They will ultimately reach about $2 trillion. That is about $8,000 for each man, woman, and child in America. Had we devoted that money to the struggle against poverty, hunger, and ill health both at home and abroad, we could have wiped out hunger, AIDS, malaria, tuberculosis, and various childhood diseases as well as illiteracy and made our world truly safer.

Even many of those who wanted us to attack Iraq, including some of our most senior military officers, now recognize that the war cannot be won. So the high costs have all been for naught. The war has been a terrible and useless waste. Instead of recognizing this fact, however, some, particularly among the so-called neoconservatives, are now in favor of what has been called the "long war" against the "universal enemy." This is a recipe for disaster. It could bring upon us, our children, and our grandchildren the nightmare described by George Orwell in his novel *1984.* Then we would not even know for what or against whom we are fighting, but in the course of fighting we would be in danger of losing the very things we are told we are fighting to preserve. Today we are truly looking into the abyss toward a hell on earth.

Changing a misguided course would not, as some have charged, be a sign of weakness that would encourage our enemies and dishearten our friends; rather, it would be a sign of strength and good sense. It is neither wise nor patriotic to continue an ill-conceived blunder that is wasting the lives of young American soldiers and Iraqi civilians while threatening the moral and fiscal integrity of the nation we all love. It is now a matter of great urgency, in the interests of both the United States and Iraq, for us to begin systematically bringing our troops home and starting the healing process.

President Bush has said, "You're either for us or against us." The authors of this book are emphatically "for us." Both of us have spent years in the service of our nation. But we also emphatically believe that true patriotism is not, as Bush has suggested, blind acquiescence to a misguided policy. Rather, it imposes on citizens the requirement to seek with intelligence, knowledge, and sound reasoning a clear view of reality. Public opinion polls tell us that Americans are trying to do so.

This book aims to help.

So much false information has been given out that the intelligent citizen is hard pressed to get a true picture of reality. So we begin our book with a summary of how Americans were misled into this needless war. Then we turn to "damage reports" on the effects of the war—on Americans, on Iraqis, and on the U.S. position in world affairs. Citizens have what government officials term a "need to know" this information in order to judge the plan we propose to get the United States out of Iraq. But those who believe they know enough about what has happened may wish to fast-forward to Chapter 5, where we lay out our plan on how to stop the hemorrhaging and get out of Iraq with the least possible cost and damage. In Chapter 6 we consider what will happen if the United States foolishly decides to "stay the course," and finally we point up the lesson that our country should learn from this costly misadventure.

George S. McGovern
William R. Polk

CHAPTER 1

How Can Citizens Find Out What They Need to Know?

"NEED TO KNOW" is a term used in the American government to segregate information. The person without a need to know a given piece of information is denied access to it; the person with the need to know—in order to perform his duties—can gain access. In order to perform our duties as citizens, we have the "need to know" what our government is doing in our names, as well as a reasonable amount of the information (or intelligence) upon which it has based its actions, and the results of those actions. We also have a legitimate need for the government to tell us honestly its best estimate of how much the implementation of its decisions will cost and what the chances of success or failure are. Most important of all, we have the right to be told the truth. But a survey by Public Agenda in January 2006 showed that half of the American public believe they were not told the truth about the Iraq invasion. Only when we have access to accurate information can we act as responsible citizens in a democratic society. As Thomas Jefferson warned, "If a nation expects to be ignorant and free . . . it expects what never was and never will be." So this chapter will highlight what Americans have been told, what has been withheld from us, what we have been falsely told, and what we have now found out.

■   ■   ■

The Iraq war has dominated television screens, newspaper headlines, and magazine articles virtually every day for the past three years. The profusion of government pronouncements, official dispatches, and images generated by photo opportunities is staggering. But the effect of this deluge of material has been less clarifying than confusing. Official proclamations have often been shortly followed by retractions; projections have been dramatically altered; and certainties quickly denied. The confusion began when neoconservatives Deputy Secretary of Defense Paul Wolfowitz and Chairman of the Defense Policy Board Richard Perle told us the 2001 attack on the World Trade Center was the work of Saddam Hussein. Secretary of Defense Donald Rumsfeld said the administration had "bulletproof" evidence that Saddam was working closely with al-Qaeda terrorists. The proof he offered, the "smoking gun," was that Saddam had an intelligence agent meet with al-Qaeda's representative in Prague. But the Czech Republic's then-president Václav Havel warned President Bush that no such meeting had taken place; American intelligence confirmed his statement and found that the alleged terrorist agent was actually in America at the time; and the 9/11 Commission reported that there was no evidence for any link between al-Qaeda and Iraq. In fact, Saddam and Osama bin Laden were bitter enemies: in 1990 Osama had even offered to raise a Muslim force to drive the *kafir*

(Arabic for "disbeliever") Saddam out of Kuwait. As much as we hated Saddam, Osama hated him even more. But President Bush and Vice President Dick Cheney continued to assert that the two were in league. Understandably, Americans are confused and misinformed. Today public opinion polls show that about one in three still believes that Saddam was involved in the 9/11 attacks.

Iraqi unmanned drone aircraft, President Bush warned us on October 7, 2002, could be used to attack America, spraying our cities with deadly germs or poison gas. But America is at least six thousand miles from Iraq, and the drone aircraft, modified Czech L-29 trainers, had a maximum range of only three hundred miles. A senior U.S. Air Force intelligence analyst, moreover, had reported *a year earlier* that the Iraqis had abandoned the program to adapt them even for aerial surveillance. They had no possible use in biological warfare.

Americans were then terrified to learn that Saddam definitely had "the bomb." National Security Council director Condoleezza Rice conjured the image of a mushroom cloud over America. That image was given substance when Vice President Cheney announced, "Simply stated, there is no doubt that Saddam Hussein now has weapons of mass destruction," and White House spokesman Ari Fleischer declared shortly before the invasion that "we know for a fact that there are [nuclear] weapons there." Secretary of Defense Rumsfeld joined the chorus, saying, "It is clear that the Iraqis have weapons of mass destruction." If any doubt remained, President Bush dispelled it by saying on May 29, 2003—that is, after the invasion, when we had inspectors on the ground—that the weapons had actually been found. On April 12, 2006, the White House admitted that when the president said this, he *already* had been briefed by his intelligence officers that the information was false, yet he and other officials continued to repeat the charge for months. Then in his State of the Union address in January 2004 the president dropped that charge but brought forth another charge: Saddam had tried to acquire uranium oxide from Africa to make a nuclear bomb. America, he and other members of his team said, had documents to prove it.

A short examination showed that the "proof" documents were actually crude forgeries, with letterheads photocopied onto new pages that had been "signed" by a minister who had left office a decade earlier. This "yellowcake scandal" spread from Rome (where the evidence had been fabricated) to Vienna (where it was unmasked) to Washington (where the attempt to deal with it has led to criminal charges against a senior member of the administration). As the American ambassador who investigated the story concluded, Saddam was not buying such materials. Indeed, he could not. According to the July 3, 2006 *National Journal,* President Bush was so infuriated that, as he admitted to federal prosecutors, he directed Vice President Cheney to discredit the messenger who had brought the unwelcome news, Ambassador Wilson.

Next came the discovery of aluminum tubes, which Vice President Cheney told us "with absolute certainty" were intended for uranium centrifuges crucial to making a nuclear weapon. When reporters asked U.S. Department of Energy engineers if these tubes could have been used for centrifuges, the engineers replied that the tubes could not. The story was a hoax.

Almost worse than nuclear weapons, as Secretary of State Colin Powell told the UN Security Council on February 6, 2003, American intelligence had discovered Iraqi mobile laboratories that were used for making horrible biological warfare materials—they were capable of producing enough anthrax or botulinum toxin to kill "thousands upon thousands of people." Later the "mobile laboratories" proved to be just pumping stations, probably intended to fill balloons with hydrogen for meteorological measurements. In the same high-tech briefing, Secretary Powell also showed slides of nuclear "decontamination vehicles" that turned out to be fire engines. Powell certainly thought that much of the intelligence on which he relied was, as he confided at the time to an aide, "bullshit," but as a "good soldier" he had presented it. A year later, in May 2004, he apologized for misleading the nation.

The list could go on.

Are all these falsehoods just mistakes? The evidence suggests that they were part of a deliberate campaign to alter the findings of the intelligence evaluation officers of the CIA, the State Department's Bureau of Intelligence and Research, and the Department of Defense's Defense Intelligence Agency. Not only did senior administration officials, including Vice President Cheney, attempt to get analysts to alter their judgments to certify what they did not believe to be true, but when those analysts did not do so to the degree demanded, the Department of Defense set up a separate organization, the Office of Special Plans, to bypass these seasoned experts and justify the decisions the administration had already made.

This charge is serious because with this bogus intelligence analysis the administration convinced the American people to support its plan to go to war and because, as Senator John Tower (R–Texas), who had investigated the Iran-Contra scandal in November 1987, sharply warned: "The democratic processes . . . are subverted when intelligence is manipulated to affect decisions by elected officials and the public."

President Bush came close to granting that that was what he was doing. In his meeting with British prime minister Tony Blair in the Oval Office on January 31, 2003, nearly three months before the U.S. invasion of Iraq, President Bush acknowledged that Iraq had no weapons of mass destruction and that he was searching for a pretext to justify the attack to the American people. One way, he suggested, would be to fly an American aircraft painted with UN insignia over Iraq; if the Iraqis fired on it, they would be in breach of UN resolutions, thereby justifying an attack;* Such moves, of course, do not fool the opponent, who after all knows what he is doing, but they can fool the American public, which must trust its public servants.

In short, as Senator Tower warned, such misinformation endangers our very system of government.

When the war began, Vice President Cheney assured us, smiling Iraqis would greet our troops as liberators. The administration's then-favored expert on Iraq, Kanan Makiyah, promised they would do so with flowers in their hands. (America was to have bad luck with its anointed Iraqis.) The war was declared over in a matter of days. Shock and awe had prevailed. "Mission accomplished," the president announced to great fanfare in the most spectacular photo-op in memory, on the deck of the aircraft carrier *Abraham Lincoln* on May 1, 2003, off the beaches of sunny California.

But soon Makiyah's flowers turned into bombs and Cheney's

---

* Senior British officials accompanying Blair wrote a memo of the talk. It was reported by Don Van Natta, Jr., in *The New York Times* of March 27, 2006, having been authenticated by two senior Foreign Office officials.

smiles into scowls of rage. Not to worry—that was just a temporary setback, President Bush assured the American public. A "few diehard Baathists" were still causing trouble, but Vice President Cheney assured us and repeated as late as in March 2005 that the insurgency was in its "last throes." The last throes lasted a long time. A year later, on March 13, 2006, President Bush said, "I wish I could tell you that the violence is waning and that the road ahead will be smooth. It will not. There will be more tough fighting and more days of struggle, and we will see more images of chaos and carnage in the days and months to come." "Days and months" soon morphed into years. How many? Some predicted five years, or perhaps ten, maybe twenty, and hopefully not more than forty.* The then-chairman of the Joint Chiefs of Staff, General Richard Myers, said that American casualties would be "reasonable." In March 2003 the Pentagon issued a directive ordering that "there will be no arrival ceremonies of, or media coverage of, deceased military personnel returning to or departing from" military bases; thereafter the wounded and coffins of the dead were kept as far as possible out of range of cameras. To avoid publicity, President Bush did not attend soldiers' funerals, as previous presidents had done.

War also costs money, of course, but the costs would be just a

---

* It is perhaps worth recalling that the "brief police action" ordered by President Harry Truman against North Korea on June 30, 1950, still has 40,000 American troops deployed along the 38th parallel that divides North and South Korea fifty-six years later. Few of these troops had yet been born when their fathers or grandfathers were dispatched to Korea at midpoint of the last century. An even larger American army has remained in Germany since World War II.

few billion dollars. On February 28, 2003, just before the invasion, Deputy Defense Secretary Wolfowitz told a House subcommittee that "containing" Saddam Hussein for the previous twelve years had cost just over $30 billion. We now know that the actual cost was at least ten times that amount. "I can't imagine anyone here wanting to spend another $30 billion to be there for another twelve years," he added. Indeed, he said, we really wouldn't need to spend *anything* because Iraq could pay for the occupation and reconstruction itself through oil sales. In fact, the American price tag for the war and occupation has risen to hundreds of billions of dollars and now is predicted to rise to perhaps as much as $2 *trillion*.

The deluge of information we have received from the government, much of it false or misleading, has certainly not met our need to know. As Will Rogers, America's homespun cowboy philosopher, once observed, "It ain't what people don't know that's dangerous. It's what they know that just ain't so." But other information that should have been given to the American people is being held secret. Secrecy in government affairs is like the dark matter that astronomers have theorized exists in outer space: like astronomical dark matter, political dark matter may actually make up most of reality. That reality is hard to find, but little by little parts of it are coming into view.

Perhaps the most painful set of revelations is the dirty story of kidnap ("extraordinary rendition" has entered the common vocabulary), torture, and homicide. Only recently have Americans had access to information on torture, although it has been long known to Iraqis and to America's friends in Europe, Africa, and Asia. Less painful or immoral but also illegal is the unexplained disappearance of about $9 billion in Iraqi money that had been held in escrow by the

UN and was then turned over to the American authorities in May 2003 for the benefit of the Iraqi people with the proviso that it be supervised by a board of independent overseers. The board was not constituted until a year later, but the money has now apparently been lost. Then there were "sweetheart" deals—like the one for $2.4 billion that was awarded without competitive bid to a subsidiary of Halliburton, the company of which Cheney was formerly chairman and from which he still draws money. After the deal was repeatedly denounced as shady and more than $1 billion of questionable charges were discovered by U.S. audits, the Army finally announced in July 2006 that it was discontinuing that contract.* Information on such affairs is not "sensitive" as an aspect of national security but is embarrassing to the administration, so where possible it is kept "dark"— that is it is classified secret, top secret, or beyond. Documents that were once open to the public have been reclassified deeper into secrecy, and thousands of others have been destroyed.

Even daily news stories from Iraq are limited and skewed in ways that we cannot judge. The press traditionally has been America's independent source of information, but at least some reporters have now traded their independence for "access." The term "embedded" came into common usage. As the Israeli journalist and former Knesset member Uri Avnery wrote on February 4, 2003, "A journalist who lies down in the bed of an army unit becomes a voluntary slave. He is attached to the commander's staff, led to the places the commander is interested in, sees what the commander wants him to see, is turned away from the places the commander does not want

* "Army to End Expansive, Exclusive Halliburton Deal," *Washington Post,* July 12, 2006.

him to see, hears what the army wants him to hear and does not hear what the army does not want him to hear. He is worse than an official army spokesman, because he pretends to be an independent reporter." Expressing his concern over the term "embedded journalists," Walter Cronkite said it "sounds too much like being in bed with the military."

Few reporters went to Iraq knowing the local language, and so they could not hope to get the opinions and observations of most Iraqis. We tend to accept this fact as a given, because Arabic is a difficult language known to few Americans, but we should ask ourselves how we would rate reports on American political affairs written by a Chinese journalist who could not speak or read English.

Language was not the only inhibitor of contact with Iraqis. The danger of leaving the fortified American city, the "Green Zone" in the center of Baghdad, has virtually prevented independent observation. The audacious reporter Robert Fisk of the *Independent* of London commented that Western correspondents have been reduced to practicing "hotel journalism." After making a trip to Iraq, the dean of an American journalism school observed that "journalists find themselves hunkered down inside whatever bubbles of refuge they have managed to create" and on their infrequent forays go surrounded by armed guards in "hardened" vehicles. A *Wall Street Journal* reporter, Farnaz Fassihi, lamented, "Being a foreign correspondent in Baghdad these days is like being under virtual house arrest . . . I avoid going to people's homes and never walk in the streets. I can't go grocery shopping anymore, can't eat in restaurants, can't strike up a conversation with strangers, can't look for stories, can't drive in anything but a full armored car, can't go to scenes of breaking news stories, can't be stuck in traffic, can't speak English outside, can't take a road trip, can't say I'm an American, can't linger at checkpoints, can't be curious about what people are saying, doing, feeling. And can't and can't . . ." *Guardian* correspondent Maggie O'Kane admitted, "We no longer know what is going on, but we are pretending we do." Even more disturbing was a report from Mark Danner in *The New York Review of Books*. "The correspondent you watch signing off his nightly report from the war zone with his name, network, and dateline Baghdad," he wrote, "is usually speaking from the grounds or the roof of a fully guarded, barricaded hotel—and may not have ventured out of that hotel all day . . . When he does leave the hotel, it will be in an armored car, surrounded by armed security guards, and very likely the destination will be a news conference or briefing or arranged interview in the vast American-ruled bunker known as 'the Green Zone.' " But despite their caution, at least sixty-one journalists have been killed since the U.S. invasion; so the Americans and British reporters increasingly "outsource" their reporting to local "stringers." The stringers are brave men, but, when we read the account of a reporter on whom we have learned to rely, we now know that often he is, in turn, relying on someone else whom we cannot know. One correspondent who was leaving Iraq commented that he was doing so because claiming to "cover" news in Baghdad was "no longer honest work."

Those reporters who have risked their lives to inform us often find that their publishers are not keen to hear what they have to report. The *New York Times* and the *Washington Post* have both admitted that they were neither sufficiently receptive to what their more independent correspondents were reporting nor critical enough of the fact that some reporters had lost their independence and had virtually become government spokesmen. When the *Wall Street Journal*'s Baghdad correspondent was too critical of the administration, the newspaper reassigned her. Helen Thomas, a Hearst newspaper columnist and dean of the White House press corps, was scathing about her colleagues. "The media," she said, "became an echo chamber for White House pronouncements."

The opposite poles in television reporting on Iraq have been Fox News and the Qatar-based news station Al-Jazeera. Fox made itself virtually a subsidiary of the military press office in Qatar and later in Baghdad, whereas Al-Jazeera made itself a pebble in the military boot. As *Newsweek* commented, "Al-Jazeera is to the Iraq war what CNN was to the gulf war—the primary source for news worldwide." So infuriating was its coverage that President Bush discussed with Prime Minister Blair his desire to bomb the Al-Jazeera station. Mr. Blair said that he dissuaded him. But in fact American forces *twice* bombed the offices of Al-Jazeera, once in Afghanistan and once in Iraq, where they killed a journalist. The military explanation was that both were mistakes, despite the fact that Al-Jazeera had informed the appropriate officials exactly where its offices were located. American troops also arrested and briefly imprisoned twenty-one of the station's employees and reporters. It also arrested, sent to the Abu Ghraib prison, and tortured an Al-Jazeera cameraman and a reporter, raided and sealed the network's Baghdad office, and banned the station from broadcasting from Iraq. Finally, one after another, senior Bush administration officials including the vice president, the secretary of defense, and the secretary of state pressured the station's owner, the tiny Gulf state of

Qatar—which hosts the main American base in the area—to close it down.*

Why did Al-Jazeera so infuriate the American command? As the American "proconsul" L. Paul Bremer III makes clear in *My Year in Iraq,* it reported unfavorable events. During one of the epic urban battles, the siege of Fallujah, he wrote, "as the fighting increased, casualties mounted and Al-Jazeera documented each one." Worse, the station even broadcast an interview with the Jordanian terrorist Abu Musab al-Zarqawi. In short, Al-Jazeera was, in the government view, a "loose cannon." It was the worst offender against one of the lessons the military had learned during the Vietnam War: that what is seen on television or reported in the press is part of the battle; therefore the military should aim to control the news. In its determination to do so, the U.S. military command in Iraq imposed restrictions on reporters' conversations even with American soldiers.

Believing that they were not getting the whole story or often not even the truth, increasing numbers of Americans have done what anti-Soviet Russians did before the fall of the USSR: they have turned to informal means of communication. The Russians used mimeograph machines to circulate information among themselves in what they called *samizdat*; we turn to Internet blogs, to hear what the mainstream press is not reporting. There are now hundreds, perhaps thousands of these websites, originating on both sides of the Atlantic and even in Iraq.

Unable to control the media or the Internet, the Bush administration has manufactured news events to get its message across. On

---

* Perhaps the best short account of these events is Christian Parenti, "Al Jazeera Goes to Jail," *Nation,* March 29, 2004.

October 13, 2005, for example, President Bush went before television cameras to ask a supposedly randomly selected group of soldiers what they thought of the way the war in Iraq was going. But the sample was not random, and the soldiers' answers were rehearsed: the participants had been carefully selected, and a Pentagon official was observed coaching them before the show. On another occasion the president sought to reassure the public that he was seeking advice from highly qualified elder statesmen. Television cameras recorded him meeting with a group of former secretaries of state and other senior officials, but the meeting actually lasted just long enough— about ten minutes—for photographs to be taken. The photo-op itself was the "advice."

So how can an intelligent citizen find out what he or she needs to know in order to perform his or her civic duties? How can he or she distinguish between propaganda and fact? Can a person find ways to discover what really is happening?

The short answer is diligence and time, plus a healthy dose of skepticism. One way or another, even information that the government tries to withhold eventually leaks. Disillusioned government officials, whistleblowers, retired professionals, and even cabinet officers are eventually driven—out of patriotism or other motives—to share what they know. Sometimes the cost of speaking out is high: the careers of senior generals, intelligence officers, and diplomats have been ruined. At least one formerly highly touted supporter of the Bush administration has been fired from his job at a private think tank.* But our pluralistic society offers niches to support all opinions,

---

* Bruce Bartlett, from the National Center for Policy Analysis in Dallas.

even dissenting ones. Fortunately it is rich enough and diverse enough to tolerate and even support organizations committed to advocating their own separate agendas. Even those information sources that are not well informed offer different perspectives and diverse opinions that provoke us to educate ourselves and demand better information. More valuable are the hundreds of colleges and universities scattered across America with programs in world affairs or regional (including Middle Eastern) studies. Many of them offer extension courses and give public symposia. Their professors can point to books, articles, and maps and give synopses of history, culture, and current events. So with persistence the intelligent citizen can get at least a reasonable fix on what is happening. The challenge is to devote the time. On the Iraq war the American public and the Congress clearly did not.

The authors of this book have been disappointed in the failure of the Democratic Party—specifically its congressional members—to develop an intelligent, informed, and outspoken loyal opposition to administration policy on the bombardment, invasion, and occupation of Iraq. To be sure, twenty-two Democratic senators voted no on the war resolutions, as did 126 members of the House. Also some of the senators and representatives have spoken out forcefully against the war. But, despite individual speeches and votes, the loyal opposition, the Democratic Party, has been timid. More important, there has been no congressional investigation on the war in Iraq comparable to the extensive public hearings conducted by the Senate Foreign Relations Committee under the late Senator William Fulbright on the Vietnam War. Those hearings, which were widely reported in the press, did much to educate the Congress and the public on the realities and follies of that war. Lack of such an authoritative and sustained congressional effort has deprived the nation of much of the information and education citizens need for an objective understanding of the Iraqi issues today.

But even when joined by such outspoken Republicans as Senator Chuck Hagel, who called Iraq "an absolute replay of Vietnam," Democrats' voices have been muted. Congressional misgivings have produced nothing like the storm of opposition to the Vietnam War that erupted in Congress, on university campuses, in churches, in the press, and across the nation. Admittedly, the administration's misleading but effective marketing has sold many Americans on this war.

During the Vietnam conflict numerous young Americans opposed the war because of the military draft then operating. Free from concerns about compulsory service during the war in Iraq, young Americans and their families have seen less reason to mobilize against this war.

Political history of the period since World War II has also played a role. Unable to prevent four successive presidential elections of Franklin Roosevelt during the Great Depression and World War II, or the upset win by President Harry Truman in 1948, Republican strategists largely ceased attacking the liberal agenda of Roosevelt's New Deal and Truman's Fair Deal. Instead they turned their political fire on Democrats and liberals, claming they are "soft on communism" and more recently "soft on terrorism." Stung by these false political labels and sometimes defeated by them, many Democrats have sought to sound as belligerent and bellicose as the political propaganda directed against them.

The Democrats' effort to sound more warlike and hostile in dealing first with communism and now with terrorism has not served the American people well. What would better serve our citizens and our national interest would be a vigorous, courageous, and persistent effort by the loyal opposition to determine, and reveal to Congress, the public, and the press, the realities underlying the war.

While some outstanding reporters have raised questions and demanded answers, the press as a whole, as we have indicated, was often passive or even imposed an informal censorship on what it printed. Consequently, the public has been ill informed and the administration did not have to face the forceful opposition to its policies in Iraq that previous administrations faced on Vietnam. Since our political system was designed to enable the people to demand information and to correct wrongful policies of government, we are all the poorer for the failures of Congress and the media. Unfortunately, neither the loyal political opposition nor the press has served the nation well in the years of the war in Iraq. They have largely failed to meet the citizens' and the soldiers' right to know.

We recognize that as with the war in Vietnam many members of Congress and the press honestly support the bombardment, invasion, and occupation of Iraq. What we are concerned with here are not the honest moral standards. Some congressmen obviously believe that American officials' abusive and torturous handling of prisoners of war is justified. They were admonished by the U.S. Supreme Court in its June 29, 2006 ruling that the president cannot rise above the American Constitution.* We should bear this in mind because

---

* *Hamdan v. Rumsfeld, Secretary of Defense, et al.*

others seem ready for additional wars with Iran and North Korea. Again, the picture that is being painted for us is based on incomplete, often dubious information. We should always bear in mind, "Ye shall know the truth and the truth shall set thee free." And, we might add, promote our safety and well-being.

Regrettably, our government has not helped us find the truth. A fair description of its attitude is, "We will run the war; your job is to 'stay the course' and pay the bills." As months have turned into years since the mission was "accomplished" in May 2003, the government has repeatedly told us that light could be seen at the end of the tunnel. But what is that light? It may not be the daylight of victory but the headlight of an oncoming train loaded with men and women whom the American invasion and occupation has transformed into anti-America terrorists. How has that happened? That is the question we will answer in the following three chapters, which together constitute what intelligence officials might call "an appreciation" of what we confront and what we have to work with, of our strengths and weaknesses, of what the Iraqi people will support or fight against, of what our friends and allies will approve or disapprove, and of our own attitudes and interests. We aim at making the kind of damage assessment that a ship captain demands after a naval battle or a collision. Making a sober and realistic damage assessment will not be easy, but it is necessary if we wish to protect our nation.

CHAPTER 2

What Is Iraq, and Who Are the Iraqis?

UNDERSTANDING THE GEOGRAPHY of Iraq and the makeup of its population is necessary for grasping the changes brought about by the American-British invasion and occupation,* because the religious, cultural, and political reactions of the Iraqis to their historical experiences constitute the lens through which they see one another and us. Not understanding—nor even apparently caring about—how they see themselves and us has been one of the causes of our failure in Iraq. Even today, after three years of war, many Americans still act as though Iraq were just a faceless desert on which we could project American power to hammer its formless people into our image. Yet Iraq is one of the most ancient nations in the world, and five thousand years ago, it was the garden from which our civilization grew.

Today's Iraq is a small and remote country. About the size of Texas, it is inhabited by some 27 million people. Baghdad is roughly

---

* For more information, see William R. Polk, *Understanding Iraq* (New York: HarperCollins, 2005, 2006).

six thousand miles away from New York. Except for a narrow funnel where its rivers empty into the Persian Gulf, Iraq is landlocked and surrounded by vast deserts and rugged mountains. In ancient times and until the First World War, Europeans called the land we now know as Iraq Mesopotamia, from the Greek words meaning "between the rivers." It was an apt name because the Tigris and the Euphrates and their tributaries have always defined the country and set the pattern of the lives of the inhabitants.

In the north, the land rises into the hills and Zagros Mountains of southern Turkey and western Iran. There the climate is cool most of the year and severely cold in the winter. Blessed with relatively abundant rainfall, the inhabitants of the north are mostly settled villagers who farm the innumerable deep valleys that cut into the foothills of the mountain range. About one in every six Iraqis lives in this area. They are the Iraqi Kurds, but only some of the Kurds are Iraqi. Most Kurds actually live in the neighboring countries. About one in every five inhabitants of Turkey is Kurdish, while Kurds make up 10 percent of the populations of Iran and Syria. If they were united in one country, their "Kurdistan" would be roughly the size of California and Pennsylvania combined—that is, larger than modern Iraq (see map). The Kurds speak an Indo-European language (distantly related to English) and are heirs of a distinctive culture that sets them off from the majority populations of the four countries in which they live. Famous throughout history for their fierce struggle for independence but divided from one another by their rugged land, they have never managed to achieve unity. Those who live in Iraq today number about four million and are Muslims, mainly of the Sunni sect.

The center of Iraq is a flat plain about the size of Louisiana. Unlike the northern mountains, this area has almost no rainfall, so the population congregates in villages, towns, and cities along rivers. The Euphrates spills down from Turkey through Syria, while the Tigris rises in the Zagros Mountains along the Iranian frontier. It was to meet the challenges posed by harnessing and struggling to control these mighty rivers that early civilization—that is, organized societies with a system of record-keeping and irrigation technology—first arose in this ancient land. The struggle continues. Today's population on this central plain is almost entirely Arabic-speaking and, like the Kurds, is mainly Sunni Muslim.

In the south the Tigris and Euphrates slowly close on each other and finally join near the city of Basra. Like central Iraq the south is mainly a flat plain, but more than the center it is laced by canals between the rivers. It has always been Iraq's breadbasket and is popularly believed to have been the Garden of Eden. But throughout recorded history its inhabitants have been poor and often persecuted. In the last century many were driven down into what amounted to serfdom. Like the people of the central plain they are mainly Arabic-speaking, but the 15 million southerners are religiously and culturally influenced by neighboring Iran and like 65 million Iranians, are Shia Muslims.*

West from the Euphrates is the great desert that extends almost

---

* Sunnis are followers of the *sunna* (Arabic: "the way") of the "orthodox" sect of Islam; they form about 40 percent of the Iraqi society. Shiis (Arabic: "partisans") differ from Sunnis in being influenced by ancient Persian religion and coming from a different historical and social background. Today they make up about 60 percent of Iraqi society.

to Damascus (Syria) and Amman (Jordan) and south deep into Saudi Arabia. Having very little water, this region can be inhabited only by nomads; today it is almost uninhabited except in oases and along the Euphrates because most Bedouin have given up their traditional way of life and moved into the settled lands.

The state of Iraq, as we knew it prior to the American invasion, was constituted by Great Britain in 1921 from three provinces of the defeated Ottoman (Turkish) Empire. The peoples from the areas centered on the cities of Mosul, Baghdad, and Basra differed in their ways of earning their livelihood; in their religions, divided among Shia and Sunni Muslims, Christians, Jews, and smaller communities of other religions; and in their cultural traditions. Today roughly eight in every ten Iraqis speak Arabic and two in every ten speak Kurdish. Smaller numbers speak Persian and various "biblical" languages. The Arabic-speaking Sunnis have always had a sense of kinship with other Arab countries, while the Shiis have maintained close ties to Iran. The Kurdish-speaking population of the north has been inexorably drawn into Turkish politics or made to feel the outward thrust of Turkish nationalism.

This diversity has led many commentators to stress the "artificiality" of Iraq. They are right that the state *is* artificial but wrong in thinking that this characteristic is either determining or unique. Few of the states of the world today, other than tiny island republics, are single culturally defined societies—"nations." Most states are made up of many nations. China contains fifty-six distinct ones, Russia at least twenty, and even France, despite nearly two centuries of intense "Francization," still feels the thrust of separate nationalisms. We in America are proud of our motto *e pluribus unum,* but we have struggled far longer than Iraq has existed to emphasize our civic unity, and we are still far from united religiously, culturally, or socially. Were we put under stress comparable to what Iraq has endured, the United States might also be described as artificial. So while Iraq *is* artificial, significant influences hold it together.

Like most states Iraq is partly held together by the institutions of the state. The aggregate of markets, employment patterns, a civil service, an army, a police force, a shared medical system, roads and highways, schools, a postal system, newspapers and television, a single currency, and even sports and myriad other daily attachments and habits form a web that is resistant to change. That web can, of course, be sundered, and Iraq is today in danger of that, but over time it has endured and become strong.

Iraqis' most powerful shared emotion is antipathy to alien rule. Seldom in their history have they been left alone. What is now Iraq has been invaded and occupied, ravaged and ruled, proselytized and converted countless times. Struggle against foreigners is the unwritten national epic of the Kurds, while the Arabs have been fighting for independence for much of the last century. Consequently, like a quarrelling family, even when Arabs and Kurds, Sunnis and Shiis, townsmen and villagers, rich and poor appear to be at one another's throats, they agree on keeping foreigners out of their land. Their xenophobia did not begin—nor will it probably end—with Americans. The story is old, but recent experience forms the lens through which Iraqis, like the rest of us, see current events. For Iraqis, that period was begun by the British invasion in the First World War.

When the British invaded what would become Iraq, they knew little about the country, but they had a model that they sought to impose upon it. The model was their Indian empire. There the British had long since decided that the natives were unfit to rule themselves. What was true in India was obviously (to the English political officers who had trained in India and who accompanied the invading British troops) true in Iraq: like the wild tribesmen on the Afghan frontier, the Bedouin seemed to them rather colorful but were simply noble savages; the peasants, like their Indian counterparts, appeared pitiful, backward, and ignorant; and worst of all were those Iraqis who resembled the Indian nationalists who *thought* they could rule themselves, the Iraqis whom the British called "the town Arabs." So the British assumed "the White Man's Burden." Their attitude triggered a vast tribal rebellion in 1920. In that rebellion Sunnis and Shiis collaborated and killed 1,654 English soldiers. To put it down, Britain had to allocate more than six times as much money as it had spent to foment the Arab rebellion against the Ottoman Empire during the world war. The tribal rebellion was the reef upon which British dreams of adding Iraq to its empire were dashed.

In a famous satire on British policy that strikes a very modern note, Colonel T. E. Lawrence ("Lawrence of Arabia") wrote the London *Sunday Times* in the midst of the revolt: "Our government is worse than the old Turkish system. They kept fourteen thousand local conscripts embodied and killed a yearly average of two hundred Arabs in maintaining peace. We keep ninety thousand men, with aeroplanes, armoured cars, gunboats and armoured trains. We killed about ten thousand Arabs in this rising this summer. We cannot hope to maintain such an average: it is a poor country, sparsely peopled . . ."

The British were not moved by Iraqi casualties, but when

Lawrence added a note on the costs, to English taxpayers, he hit a nerve: "How long will we permit millions of pounds, thousands of imperial troops, and tens of thousands of Arabs to be sacrificed on behalf of a form of colonial administration . . ." The answer came soon. Under the leadership of Winston Churchill, Britain changed course—or at least changed the cosmetics of its rule. Some of its moves bear an uncanny resemblance to American actions since our invasion in 2003. First, the British gave Iraqis the facade of a native government based on a model of their own government; second, they legitimized this new regime by holding a sort of election; third, they set about winning over enough of the natives to support the regime; and fourth, they created an Iraqi army to police the country. These moves set the matrix for the next half-century of Iraq, and because they can be compared to what America is doing in Iraq today, they tell us why Iraqis have attitudes—and memories—that often surprise us. We need to understand them, so let us look briefly at the four main British policies.

The political facade that the British erected included a British-selected king whose government was composed of British-approved Iraqi ministers. Each of these men was "advised" by a British official—whose advice he had to follow. In 2003 and 2004, with the substitution of an American-style government for a British-style monarchy, this is almost exactly what L. Paul Bremer III did. To make this government seem "democratic" in the approved Western style, the British drafted an eloquent constitution, created law courts, and arranged to hold elections. Bremer did the same in the Coalition Provisional Authority (CPA).

Initially, the British creation of what they made to appear to be a native government countered Iraqi fears that Britain planned to rule Iraq. But the Iraqis were not fooled for long. As the years went by, their early fears were substantiated. In the offices of those Iraqis whom the British had selected as ministers, British officials were always just behind the curtain and always had means available to make sure their advice was followed.

The establishment of this government, the creation of a national parliament, and even the holding of elections, while done in the name of "democracy," had the effect of driving a wedge between the Sunnis and Shiis. Since the Shiis had played a major role in the 1920 revolt and had few Westernized leaders who had rapport with British officials, the British regarded them with suspicion and drew almost entirely on Sunnis to form the government. But the British recognized that excluding the Shiis provided only temporary stability; for the longer term, they knew they had to win over enough Shia leaders to control their community. They had to let Shiis into the new parliament. The parliament itself was not very important, but even so it was prudent to make sure that it not become (as the Indian parliament had already become) a forum to air dissent. Those who were elected had to be won over into complicity with British rule. So in a second, more slowly effected, and subtler stage of the imposition of their control, the British encouraged what amounted to a social revolution, whose effects have lasted to the present day.

This social revolution was aimed at Iraqi tribal society. Traditionally, the tribes had been egalitarian and communal: tribal elders, while they were respected hosts and advisers, to their kinsmen were not rulers. Nor were they usually wealthy, since tribal lands were not their property. They were literally "firsts among equals." That made them less reliable than the British wanted or thought Iraq needed. So what the British did was to "promote" (as they then said) elders into "chiefs" (a position alien to the Arab tribes), while driving down—with the help of city moneylenders and, where necessary, government troops—their Shia fellow tribesmen into serfdom. The newly created tribal chiefs took over the lands that had been tribal property and, so enriched, threw in their lot with the British-controlled, mainly Sunni, government. This shift left a residue of fear and hatred that is manifested today in the attacks on Iraqis who collaborate with the Americans.

Also detrimental to the civic health of Iraq, the policies adopted by the supposedly democratic and representative British-sponsored government tarnished those very concepts. "Democracy" became a suspect word: from the way it was practiced, it came to mean corruption, unfair privilege, and exploitation. For this turn away from real participation in government, Iraq would pay a fearful price in the next half-century. It is still doing so. And oblivious to this bit of Iraqi history, American administrators have been baffled by Iraqis' suspicion when American administrators speak to them of democracy.

The long-term costs of the British policies have been high, but from the relatively short-term British point of view, the system worked. Public order was maintained; the economy slowly grew; and everyone adjusted to the new system. Gradually the British intelligently removed as many of themselves as possible from sight: they withdrew their armed forces to more or less isolated bases, from which RAF planes could drop bombs or poison gas and from which motorized units armed with machine guns could launch occasional search-and-destroy raids, and stood ready to assume control if the Iraqi government caused them trouble. The British bases were the fist hidden inside the glove. America is today building at least four huge remote bases that could serve as springboards for military action by its air force and small mobile columns of special forces. To some Americans, these bases seem to offer a smart way to get our troops out of sight—and so out of trouble—yet keep them available on short notice. Remembering the British era, however, Iraqis view the American base policy with dread. Americans would do well to consider the fact that the creation of huge American bases in Saudi Arabia helped generate the anger that turned Osama bin Laden from a pampered millionaire into a religious terrorist.

Creation of these bases also suggests a permanent occupation. Certainly any Iraqis who read American government statements are aware that the Bush administration is considering staying in Iraq for years. Secretary of State Rice has referred to our involvement as "a generational commitment." And on the ground in Baghdad, confirmation appears in concrete. The new American embassy compound, the Green Zone, is estimated to cost up to $1 billion and will contain a small city with three hundred houses, barracks for a large Marine contingent, and twenty-one other buildings. It will have its own electrical, water, and sewage systems. Not surprisingly, most Iraqis think that the United States will never withdraw unless forced to do so. This feeling perhaps explains why a *USA Today*/CNN/Gallup poll showed that eight out of every ten Iraqis regarded America not as a "liberator" but as an occupier, and 88 percent of the Sunni Muslim Arabs favored violent attacks on American troops.

The British, like their American successors today, placed major emphasis on achieving "security," and set about creating an Iraqi army. There are compelling reasons for this policy: for one thing, ruling through natives is cheaper than ruling with imported foreigners. The British, like the Americans, also believed that native troops would be less unpopular than foreigners. That proposition is far more dubious: if native troops are perceived to be puppets of foreigners, they may be even more violently opposed than the foreigners themselves. "Iraqization," like "Vietnamization," threatens the very basis of a nationalist insurgency. Thus the insurgents regard native participants in a foreign-controlled regime as quislings. Hardly a day passes in Iraq without an insurgent attack on a police or army post. And Iraqi troops, when put to the test to support the policies set out by the Americans, often refuse to fight, or they join the insurgents. In the great urban battles for Mosul, Fallujah, Najaf, and Basra, they often simply disappeared. Foreigners usually blame the inaction of native troops on poor training or inadequate equipment; these factors may play a part, but almost certainly the troops have attitudes that no training is likely to alter while foreigners remain in Iraq.

Frustrated by the unwillingness of Arabs to act against Arabs, the British enrolled troops from one of Iraq's ethnic minorities, the Assyrians. These "levies," as the British called Assyrian troops, were kept at parity with the Iraqi army that the British had created. The Iraqis naturally regarded the Assyrians as puppets of the imperialists and, in one of their first acts upon acquiring a modicum of independence, turned on them and massacred them. Today the American military, facing the same problem the British faced, has fallen back on Kurdish paramilitary forces (Kurdish: *peshmerga*) to help them fight Arab insurgents. Inevitably this policy has contributed to today's ethnic tensions and is bound to make Iraq far less stable in the future.

More important for the health of Iraqi society is the fact that the creation of security forces is relatively simple and speedy compared with the creation of balancing civic institutions. In Iraq in the 1930s and again in the 1950s and 1960s the army was the only functioning, powerful, and mobile organization. Regarding itself as the only "pure" national institution and the only able defender of the country, time after time the army overthrew civilian governments of which it disapproved—or when its commanders grew ambitious. More important, it prevented the growth, however feeble, of an independent judiciary, a representative parliament, and a free press. Consequently Iraqi society lurched from one military dictatorship to the next with never a chance to form coherent institutions or even the accustomed habits of civil society. The British policy thus—inadvertently, to be sure—formed the basis on which the tyranny of Saddam Hussein rested. The current American emphasis on achieving "security" by creating an Iraqi army gives us every reason to believe that this pattern will repeat itself. Building a large new army today will likely once again prove a major obstacle to Iraqi stability and freedom.

Does Iraq have a chance to attain stability and freedom? Many observers today do not think so. Certainly just writing a constitution or holding elections is unlikely to effect them, but an older Iraqi tradition offers more promise. Before the British came, each neighborhood or village took responsibility for its own education, public health, and maintenance of public order, as well as the upkeep of mosques, churches, or synagogues. Even the assessment and collection of taxes was a community affair. The British found that these things were inefficiently done, but by taking them out of the hands of the inhabitants, even to improve their efficiency, they suppressed what was a kind of democracy. Although enfeebled, that tradition of popular participation in public affairs is not dead. It may offer Iraq its best hope for the future because the place to begin is at the grass-roots. Democracy is above all a learning process, and only if the Iraqi people begin to manage their own affairs will an acceptable and viable form of democracy take root.

The British did not help the Iraqis to learn; indeed, they virtually opposed education. In an early report to the League of Nations, the British high commissioner wrote that "in this country, it is neither desirable nor practicable to provide Secondary education except for the select few." In 1932, after ten years of British rule, Iraq had two thousand students in secondary schools and none in institutions of higher education. In the following period of indirect British rule, another twenty-five years passed before Iraq had fourteen thousand secondary school students. As late as 1950 the number of Iraqi men and women who had specialized skills in medicine or engineering could be counted on the fingers of one hand. More were trained in the humanities, but they rarely found an outlet for their skills other than teaching.

Even those Iraqis who hate Saddam Hussein today credit him with having reversed the policy that the British established and their Iraqi puppets carried forward: Baath rule, awful as it was in many ways, favored education, so that millions of Iraqis were educated and found outlets for modern skills in the society he helped to create. In the field of health care, for example, on the eve of the 1991 Gulf War,

Iraq had a network of eighteen hundred health care centers offering one of the most advanced systems in the Middle East. Manned by more than ten thousand doctors, its services were free. Most Iraqis would probably say today that they would like to return to Saddam's 1970s and 1980s policy of modernization, but of course without his tyranny.

Looking ahead, Iraqis fear those who may try to tread in the Anglo-American footprints. The Kurds are well aware of the hostility of the Turks, who have treated "their" Kurds with great savagery, killing more than thirty thousand of them in the 1980s, razing whole villages, and refusing to allow Kurds the right to use their own language. The Turks have periodically conducted search-and-destroy raids into Iraqi Kurdistan. They ally themselves with an Iraqi minority, the Azeri Turkmen, who make up about a third of the population of Kirkuk, to try to prevent the Kurds from taking over the nearby giant oil field; moreover, they are dead set against the creation of an independent Kurdish state in Iraq, which they believe would encourage dissidence among the Kurds living in Turkey.

The Sunni Arabs have had a love-hate relationship with other Arabs. In 1961 a predecessor of Saddam, General Abdul Karim Qasim, asserted a claim to Kuwait. His move was dramatic, but his claim was not new: every government of Iraq from 1921 believed that the British had "stolen" Kuwait from Iraq. But it was disturbing to Iraqis in Qasim's time that a coalition of other Arabs led by Egypt's great pan-Arab leader, Gamal Abdul Nasser, warned them away from Kuwait. Even today some Iraqis are fearful that both Jordan and Syria aspire to control Iraq.

The Shiis, while often dependent on the Iranians and culturally and religiously allied with them, have repeatedly demonstrated their determination to defend Iraq from Iran. They did so even on behalf of Saddam Hussein, a large part of whose army and even officer corps in the 1980–88 Iraq-Iran War was made up of Shiis.

In short, Kurds, Sunni Arabs, and Shia Arabs share a fear of their neighbors and realize that however uncomfortable was—and is—their shared membership in Iraq, anything else might be worse.

Iraq's riches in oil will intensify all these pressures on Iraq's ethnic and religious groups. For nearly a century oil has been both the blessing and the curse of Iraq. The oil industry began with a bizarre diplomatic and commercial juggling act among the European powers. The first concession to look for oil in what became Iraq was given to an Anglo-German company on June 28, 1914—remarkably, less than two months before the two countries declared war on each other. Then during the First World War, as a part of one of the most tortured diplomatic negotiations ever undertaken, the British and French agreed that what would become northern Iraq would go to France. But having already smelled oil on the site of Nebuchadnezzar's "fiery furnace" near Kirkuk, British companies got their government to pressure the French into giving up their claim. France did not have to give up much, because neither Britain nor France actually possessed the area: an Ottoman Turkish army still occupied the prospective oil field. So the British disregarded the armistice they had just concluded with Turkey and drove the Turks out. To keep them out, they agreed that Turkey would receive 10 percent of any oil discovered there for twenty-five years, and to sweeten the fait accompli for the French, they agreed that France would get roughly a quarter of any oil that might be found. No one, of course, consulted any Iraqis during these negotiations or, indeed, any others for the next forty years.

Britain's absolute insistence on controlling oil explains why it went into Iraq. If the financially troubled empire could establish a monopoly of Middle Eastern oil, British statesmen thought, it would take on a new life. Iraq was under control, and France and Turkey had been bought off. But the U.S. government also wanted in. In the early 1920s petroleum engineers believed that American reserves would run out in less than a decade. In a panic, even the very conservative Republican administrations of Presidents Warren G. Harding and Calvin Coolidge considered going into the oil business as a state enterprise. Partly to head off this swing toward "petroleum socialism," the major oil companies decided to internationalize themselves. Iraq was a prime target. So on behalf of the majors, the American government pressured the British to allow American participation. After astonishingly bitter diplomatic negotiations between these recent wartime allies, the British and American governments concluded a deal in 1925 to give two American petroleum giants, Standard Oil of New Jersey and Socony-Vacuum, roughly a quarter share in what became known as the Iraq Petroleum Company. It was this group that struck oil near Kirkuk in 1927. Iraqi oil was thereafter to be an Anglo-Franco-American monopoly. (Oil has remained the magnet that draws foreigners into Iraq up to the present moment. Almost all Iraqis—and many outside observers—believe that acquisition of Iraqi oil was a major reason for the American invasion.)*

* In 2002, just before the American invasion, only one of the world's ten most profitable corporations was in the oil and gas field; in 2005 four of the ten were. They were Exxon-Mobil and Chevron Texaco (American) and Shell and BP (British). The Iraq war doubled the price of crude; it would go up another 50 percent during the first months of 2006.

With its stake in Iraqi oil secured, America also acquired a stake in the maintenance of British hegemony in Iraq. During the Eisenhower administration the United States entered into a broad military and political alliance, commonly called the Baghdad Pact, with the government of Britain's most trusted Iraqi deputy, Prime Minister Nuri Pasha al-Said, who was almost universally hated in Iraq. Al-Said and the king were overthrown in 1958 by the Iraqi army under General Abdul Karim Qasim.*

The coup seemed to open a new era of political freedom for Iraqis, but that hope died almost before it could gain any substance. The army was interested not in freedom but only in power. The new government found no basis on which to build a consensus and lapsed into an ugly tyranny. In its turn it was overthrown, and Iraqi politics again became, as it had been in the 1930s, a game of musical chairs. After an unedifying series of coups, the winner was the group of conspirators who had formed the Baath Party, which was soon to be dominated by Saddam Hussein.

It is now not discussed much, but during the Reagan administration and the early part of the administration of George H.W. Bush, the American government had a close and supportive relationship with Saddam. The reason was that on September 22, 1980, Iraq got into a war with America's enemy, the revolutionary Islamic fundamentalist Ayatollah Khomeini, whose supporters had overthrown America's ally, the government of the shah in Iran. Having a common enemy brought Iraq and the United States into a series of rela-

* As a young congressman, George McGovern was in Iraq at this time and saw the bodies of the king and prime minister being dragged through the streets of Baghdad.

tionships that, in retrospect, seems absolutely astonishing. America was determined that Saddam not lose the war. During 1983, it began to look like he might—Iraqi troops killed in action topped 100,000 and wounded at least twice that figure, and the Iranian armed forces seemed on the point of a breakthrough. So the U.S. government supplied Saddam with up-to-the minute satellite photographs showing Iranian troop dispositions and movements, which turned the fortunes of the conflict. Further, it gave or lent Saddam's regime money and food without which the Iraqi economy might have collapsed. And it supplied or arranged for others to supply Saddam's armed forces with cluster bombs, as well as chemical and biological weapons equipment and stocks, and it even provided some help toward Iraqi acquisition of a nuclear weapon. Finally, President Ronald Reagan sent Donald Rumsfeld, his special envoy to the Middle East, to Baghdad as a public show of support for Saddam.

True, during this period there were disagreements, particularly over the use of poison gas on Kurdish villagers (which made Saddam unpopular in America) and over his support of the Palestinian struggle for independence (which made him unpopular among neoconservatives). But government-to-government relations remained cordial until two years after the war with Iran ended, when Saddam violated the absolute prohibition in Middle Eastern affairs by threatening the flow of oil.

CHAPTER 3

Effects on Iraq of the American Invasion and Occupation

THE COLLAPSE of the American relationship with Saddam Hussein began in 1990 with a curiously vague diplomatic encounter: his meeting with the U.S. ambassador. At that time Saddam's government was broke. The end of the war with Iran had brought not relief but catastrophe. Iraq needed to restart the massive social and public works programs that had invigorated Iraqi society and enriched Saddam's supporters, but once Iran was defeated, those Arab countries that had lent him money to fight Iran lost the will to continue. Kuwait not only demanded repayment of its wartime loans but drove down the price of oil by overproduction, from $21 in January 1990 to $11 a barrel six months later. At $21 a barrel the Iraqi regime could survive, but at $11 it could not. Kuwait's action was a death threat to the regime. As rumors of plots to overthrow him circulated, Saddam began to fear for his life.

It wasn't just this "dumping" of cheap oil that made Kuwait unpopular. The Iraqis had always regarded Kuwait as an outpost of British imperialism and charged that it had been taken away from them by the British imperialists. The way the frontier had been drawn, they maintained, choked Iraq's access to the Persian Gulf. Iraqis were also jealous: Kuwait, a state about the size of Connecticut with a population smaller than that of Dallas, had become incredibly rich after oil production began in the 1950s. As seen from Baghdad, Kuwait was nothing but a huge oil field topped by banks full of money. Those assets had been crucial to Iraq's survival in the war with Iran, and Saddam thought they were the key to the survival of his regime. To try to resolve the issues of debt and the level of oil production, Saddam turned to Jordan's King Hussein, Egypt's President Hosni Mubarak, and Saudi Arabia's King Fahd. They offered to mediate, but Kuwait turned them down. Saddam could count his days. Furious and fearful, he decided to seize the oil fields and rob the bank—Kuwait.

Before doing so, he prudently sounded out the United States. The signals he got were at least neutral. In Washington a spokesman for the State Department said, "We do not have any defense treaties with Kuwait, and there are no special defense or security commitments to Kuwait." To be sure he had heard correctly, Saddam called in the American ambassador to Iraq, April Glaspie. What, he wanted to know, was the stance of her government toward the Kuwait-Iraq issue? Possibly a clear and forceful statement that America would protect Kuwait would have warned him off, but she did not give it. The view of the American government, astonishingly, was that the issue was not money or oil but a small disputed strip of desert along the frontier between Kuwait and Iraq. Addressing that issue and under clear instructions from Washington, the ambassador told Saddam that America took no position on border disputes among Arab states. The ambassador's message was reconfirmed by the assistant secretary of state in testimony before a congressional committee on July 31, 1990. Saddam thought he had seen a green light, and on August 2, he ordered his army to invade, quickly overwhelmed the Kuwait forces, and proclaimed Kuwait "again" a province of Iraq.

In public at least, the American response was surprise. Reflecting on Saddam's attack later, Ambassador Glaspie said that no one in the American government had thought Saddam was going to take *all* of Kuwait but only the disputed strip. (Presumably, the first Bush administration would have allowed him to take just that strip.) But nothing Saddam heard indicated that attitude: he assumed that the United States would protest but that the protest would be only pro forma; then America and the other powers would accept the facts on the ground.

Understandably, in the Middle East, where motives are usually taken at their worst, many people thought that the Bush administration had baited a trap for Saddam. Certainly he was astonished at the speed and clarity of the American reaction. Some even thought it had been prepared in advance. The United States immediately secured a unanimous Security Council resolution demanding Iraqi withdrawal. More ominous to Iraq was the fact that the Soviet Union joined America in denouncing Saddam's invasion. Then followed a confused period of attempts to cool down the crisis: proposals were put forward by Iraq, Russia, the various Arab states, France, and Yugoslavia—all to be rejected by the United States. It has since been reported that General Colin Powell, then the chairman of the Joint Chiefs, favored giving the Arab governments six months time to work out a solution to the Iraq-Kuwait crisis. Powell's position was known to a few U.S. senators, including the influential Georgia senator Sam Nunn, chairman of the Senate Armed Services Committee, who offered this alternative to the Senate against the administration's demand for an immediate war authorization. By a margin of only one vote, the Senate yielded to the Bush administration position in favor of war unless the Iraqis withdrew their forces from Kuwait in short order.

The United States prepared for war. The first step was logistical, to get Saudi Arabia to "request" that American troops be stationed in that country. (Their intrusion into the Islamic "holy land," we have seen, was the action that infuriated Muslim fundamentalists like Osama bin Laden and laid the groundwork for the rise of Islamic fundamentalist terrorism.) By the end of the year America had stationed nearly a quarter of a million troops, at least a thousand aircraft, and thirty missile-armed naval ships within range of Iraq. Allies—including other Arab states and Turkey—were rounded up, convinced, or bribed. On November 29, 1990, at the urging of the United States, the UN Security Council authorized "all necessary means" to force Iraq out of Kuwait and set a deadline of January 15, 1991, for compliance. Saddam refused to yield. He probably hoped that the unlikely coalition that America had cobbled together would fall apart. Almost certainly he believed that if he capitulated, he would be overthrown and murdered by his own army.

The American attack began on January 17. It was more massive than any prior military engagement in history: Iraq was blasted by 88,000 tons of bombs dropped by wave after wave—more than 100,000 sorties—of aircraft and nearly three hundred missiles.

Against the American juggernaut, the Iraqi army was unable to protect even itself. The combat was not so much a war as, in the then-current description, a "turkey shoot." In impotent fury, the Iraqis vented their frustration and anger on Kuwait by setting its oil fields afire. That diversion did not stop the Americans, so Saddam gave up on February 27, and President Bush, to the fury of his neoconservative advisers, ordered a cease-fire.

Saddam's decision ended the American-Iraqi war, but it also created conditions for a dreadful civil war. Encouraged by the United States, the long-suppressed Shia population of southern Iraq rose in revolt. For reasons that are still unclear, having incited them, the United States not only allowed Saddam's army to attack the Shiis with helicopter gunships and to pass armored columns through American lines but even protected arms dumps from the rebels who were trying to obtain the means to defend themselves. The result was a massacre. By the end of March thousands of Shiis had been killed, their property destroyed, and their revolt crushed. Worse—if anything could have been worse—Saddam decided to effect a plan that had long been studied by various Iraqi governments: to drain the marshes, an area the size of New Jersey formed by the Tigris and Euphrates rivers, just north of Basra. Ostensibly, doing so would benefit agriculture and improve health, but Saddam's real motivation, no doubt, was to deprive Shia rebels of their final refuge. It was Iraq's equivalent of defoliation in Vietnam. It was an ecological as well as a human disaster.

Meanwhile, in the north, the Kurds also had taken advantage of the Kuwait war to rebel. Their most important objective was the Kirkuk oil field, which, presumably, they thought they could use as a bargaining chip to achieve autonomy. But Saddam was too quick for them. Even though much of his army and virtually all of his air force had been destroyed, he struck the Kurds with overwhelming force. When their lightly armed militia tried to retreat, the Turks closed the frontier. At least on the Kurdish issue, Turkey agreed with Saddam: Kurdish desires for independence must be crushed. Despairing, the Kurds withdrew from Kirkuk into their mountains. There they were to remain for the next decade.

How to punish and weaken Iraq was the question the victors raised. Led by the United States, they arranged in April 1991 that the Security Council impose a program of sanctions. Iraq was to give up work on weapons of mass destruction under the supervision of foreign inspectors, who were to be backed up by the threat of air strikes for noncompliance. More important in its effects on Iraqi society, the country's assets abroad were frozen and almost all imports (including foodstuffs and medicines) and exports (including oil) were banned. Those Americans who favored sanctions pointed out that imposing them upon Iraq would at least prevent Iraq from recovering its ability to make war and at best might cause the Iraqi people or army to overthrow Saddam's detested regime. Critics have pointed out that the sanctions regime was the most draconian measure ever imposed upon a defeated power since Rome defeated Carthage—far more punitive than those imposed upon defeated Germany or Japan at the end of the Second World War. What soon became evident was that Iraq had no internationally significant military capacity left, so the sanctions were probably irrelevant, but that, since the regime was strong enough and determined enough to protect at least itself and its adherents, the effects of the sanctions would fall on the weaker members of the society. The sanctions program, although eased in the later 1990s, remained in effect until the American invasion in 2003 and drastically affected the health of a whole generation of Iraqis.

Despite rationing, food supplies dwindled so that roughly a quarter of all children between the ages of six months and five years were found to suffer from chronic malnutrition. This rate is comparable to that of Burundi, an African nation that has been ravaged by more than a decade of war. Chronic malnutrition shows up particularly in what is called stunting (the child fails to grow proportional to its age) and in wasting (the child is excessively underweight for its height and age). Stunting and/or wasting affected about one in every four Iraqi children. By 1993 sanctions had caused the deaths of an estimated half a million Iraqi children. On the CBS news program *60 Minutes* the American ambassador to the UN, Madeleine Albright, was told that this was more children than died in Hiroshima. When asked, "Is the price worth it?" she replied, "We think the price is worth it."

In addition to widespread malnutrition, large numbers of Iraqis were affected by another consequence of the war. With effects not then realized, the depleted uranium artillery shells and bombs used by American forces left a deadly legacy even beyond the fighting— a greatly increased incidence of cancer.

Iraq hit bottom in 1994. Unable to sell its goods abroad and having no money to buy what it needed from other countries, the modern economy that Saddam had built before the ruinous war with Iran and the ill-advised invasion of Kuwait simply petered out. Hospitals ran out of even soap to wash bedding and could no longer use

sophisticated diagnostic and therapeutic equipment for lack of supplies and spare parts. Antibiotics and anaesthetics became unobtain-
able. Even bandages had to be reused. Alarming accounts of these
dire conditions began to circulate among the victors. Particularly the
effects of malnutrition—literally the starving of the Iraqi population—began to be publicized. Soon they were so alarming that public pressure built up to remove the sanctions. The result was the 1995
Oil for Food program.

Under the strict supervision of an American-led committee
under the UN, Iraq was to be allowed to export small amounts of oil
in order to purchase such foodstuffs and medicines as the committee
approved. Initially the impact of imported food and medical goods
was small. A careful United Nations Development Program study
pointed out that by 1996 "nearly one-third of hospital beds were
closed, more than half of the hospital equipment did not work, and
many departments did not have a functioning toilet." Although
somewhat eased eventually, the sanctions program would remain in
effect until the American invasion seven years later.

Since the publicly proclaimed purpose of the sanctions was to
destroy the Iraqi regime, that regime tried to protect itself both by
evading the restrictions and by using such revenues as it had to rebuild its security forces. If Saddam's government had any doubts
about the intent of the Western powers, it was frequently reminded
by the constant overflight of its territory, the banning of its aircraft
from all but a central strip of the country, and occasional bombings
and missile attacks. These separate actions were disturbing, but they
did not add up to a coherent and effective policy: the Iraqi regime did
not collapse, the Iraqi people suffered (during the sanctions era, in

overall terms of health, education, and development, according to UNICEF, Iraq fell from 50th to 126th out of 130 countries), and the surrounding countries, allies of the United States, lost major sources of revenue when oil ceased to flow through their territories and the Iraqis could not buy their goods. Unofficially and covertly, under the leadership of the United States, the sanctions were eased. In fact, according to a U.S. Senate report, the major purchasers of the heavily discounted Iraqi oil were American oil companies whose purchases were occasionally facilitated by the U.S. government. These purchases further undermined the declared American policy by yielding kickbacks to Saddam Hussein's regime.

At the end of 1996 Iraq was allowed to export oil; by 1998 it was exporting $10.5 billion worth. Controls were then completely lifted, so that by 2000 Iraq was earning more than $30 billion from oil exports. The economy began to recover. War damage was being repaired: Iraqis were proud that they had rebuilt a symbol of their modernity, the grand bridge across the Tigris at Baghdad. The electrical grid that had been severely damaged in the 1991 war was restored so that clean drinking water became available and sewage could be treated. And Saddam, reassured by his growing capacity, again indulged in his passion, so reminiscent of Mussolini and Hitler, for grandiose architecture: Baghdad blossomed with arches and statues.

But underneath these manifestations of the staying power of the Baath regime were warnings of its weakness. Perhaps the most important was the steady emigration of the educated elite portion of the population. Tens of thousands of the very people Iraq most needed left the country. Some went because the sanctions regime had destroyed the outlets for their skills (this was particularly true among doctors and engineers), while others saw no hope for "the good life" in an Iraq beset by foreigners and ruled by a tyrant. As schools were closed and teachers dispersed, the literacy rate for the coming generation fell. Even the Baath Party, theretofore Saddam's base of power, was affected. As rumors of dissatisfaction reached his ears, he came to trust the party less and less. So to supplement, balance, or replace it, he resurrected the British system of "promoting" tribal chiefs. Long regarded as enemies of progress and of the regime, they were again courted and given money and deeds to still more land (or lands that had been nationalized earlier). Almost overnight those who had been treated as mere antiques were once again in favor. What was politically significant was that, feeling threatened by nearly the entire society, Saddam fell back upon a kinship system that predated Islam. That is, he came to rely not on his political organization, the Baath Party, or on the balance he created among the several security organizations, or on the wider circle of supporters on whom he had lavished government contracts, but only on his immediate kinsmen, his clan, the Al Majid. As heir to the ancient Arab tradition, he viewed the clan as the ultimate repository of loyalty: all its members were responsible for one another's actions, and each was absolutely required to protect or avenge all. This was one tradition that had remained intact throughout Iraqi history, and it is still a force with which America must reckon today. For Saddam, his clan was his final redoubt.

So it was that, driven to the wall by his defeat in the Kuwait war, shaken by the Shia and Kurdish revolts, and distrustful, even of his own political organization, he resurrected (although he probably did not make the historical connection) the most primitive of all

Arab political ideas, the primacy of close kinship. He quickly applied it to his government, security organizations, and army. From then on it was kinship, not skill, that counted. So it came as a profound shock to him and to his clan when in 1995 his sons-in-law fled Iraq with his two daughters and their children. What was even more disturbing to Saddam was that one of the sons-in-law, General Husain Kamil, was the head of Iraq's weapons program. He was inadvertently to play a key role in the buildup to the 2003 American attack. In his refuge in Jordan, General Kamil was interviewed by Western intelligence agents. There he was quoted asserting that Saddam had a vigorous program to develop weapons of mass destruction. Nothing else that he could have said could have had more impact, because the issue of weapons by then had become the flashpoint of Iraqi-American relations. American intelligence officers and nongovernmental "experts" (especially in the enormously influential neoconservative movement) believed or at least charged that Saddam was trying covertly to acquire weapons of mass destruction. There was logic to the charge: as a senior Israeli intelligence officer commented, Saddam would have been a fool not to do so because, already in 1991, the American government was openly discussing how to kill him. Both President George H.W. Bush and President Clinton had avidly searched for proof that he was violating the restrictions on weapons, so they would have an excuse to depose him. Unquestionably Saddam would have liked to have the security given by possession of the ultimate weapon, a nuclear bomb, but he was smart enough to know that during the period of trying to acquire one, a regime is highly vulnerable to attack. So apparently he decided that, at least for the moment, he could not risk the attempt. In fact, as was later admitted, Saddam's son-in-law, General Kamil, actually had told Western intelligence agents that the program to acquire such weapons had been abandoned.

What emerges from a close reading of the events of the 1990s is a series of attempts to find Saddam guilty of almost anything that would justify an attack on his regime. One incident that happened in 1993 would arise again a decade later, when President George W. Bush remarked that "Saddam tried to kill my dad." What happened has never been satisfactorily explained but the most convincing interpretation is that the plot was probably fictitious.* What was important about it, and the attempt to use Saddam's son-in-law as a witness against him, was that they probably convinced Saddam that no matter what he did or did not do, America was intent on destroying him. If he needed more proof, he got it when his security organization penetrated one of the dissident groups financed by the CIA. The Iraqi National Accord was being paid to carry out car bomb attacks and assassinations of Baathist officials and ultimately of Saddam. (That group was headed by a former Baathist, Iyad al-Allawi, who later became the first American-appointed Iraqi prime minister.)

After this decade-long series of threats, destabilization programs, covert assassination attempts, and aerial assaults, the event that finally justified the 2003 invasion was the attack on the World Trade Center and the Pentagon, in which—ironically, because there was so much for which to blame the Saddam regime—the Iraqis played no part.

---

* It is briefly discussed in William R. Polk, *Understanding Iraq* (New York: HarperCollins, 2005, 2006), 162–63.

The 2003 American-British attack on Iraq was far more massive and destructive than the 1991 invasion by the first Bush administration. "Shock and awe" aptly summarizes its meaning. Some 37,000 air sorties by the U.S. Air Force dropped 13,000 "cluster munitions" that exploded into two million cluster bombs, wiping out whole areas. Aircraft fired 23,000 missiles, while naval ships loosed 750 cruise missiles that delivered another 1.5 million pounds of explosives. The weight of artillery shells fired is not recorded, but the aggregate air and land strikes are estimated to have resulted in well over $100 billion worth of physical damage. No exact figures will ever be known, but at least ten thousand civilians—including about three thousand children—and scores of thousands of Iraqi soldiers were killed in the first twenty-one days of fighting.

Statistics are one of the subterfuges of war. They neither illustrate the suffering nor explain the extent of damage. Most accounts of warfare in the past have emphasized the colorful, the glorious, the brave. Tennyson and Kipling gave us an image of war that was almost attractive. In modern warfare, when the combatants are usually far apart and rarely even see their targets, we take refuge from reality in phrases like "surgical strikes," but, occasionally eyewitnesses bring out the human dimension of war. In the 2003 Iraq war the most graphic reports were those of the English journalist Robert Fisk.* The war he reported was one not of surgical strikes but of suffering people and mutilated bodies. He reported what so many Iraqis saw at first hand. And in that small country practically every family had a relative, a neigh-

* Focus: Part One, The Human Cost—"Does Tony Have Any Idea What the Flies Are Like That Feed Off the Dead?" *Independent*, January 26, 2003.

bor, or a friend who had been wounded or killed. Later, as it came back into operation, Iraqi television began to show scenes of horror from the great battles for Iraq's cities. Nothing on American television equalled what became almost daily fare for the Iraqis: Americans and Iraqis saw quite different "realities," quite different wars.

In the fighting the Iraqis were outgunned, outfought, and outled. They never had a chance. Their army was shattered, and as a 2005 UN Development Program (UNDP) study determined, roughly a quarter of a million people contracted "a chronic health problem directly caused by war . . . more children, elderly, and women have been disabled than in previous wars." The electrical system was a prime target, and—ironically, because the infrastructure of Iraq had become sophisticated, centralized, and modernized under Saddam—it cracked under the shock of the attack. Large parts of the country were left in darkness and without access to clean drinking water—the UNDP study estimated that roughly three-quarters of a million Iraqi households had unsafe and unstable drinking water—and even in the cities a large portion of the population had no means to dispose safely of sewage. The combination of these effects soon caused deaths by diarrhea to surge from two to four out of every ten. Not much could be done for the ailing because during the invasion, about half of the eighteen hundred primary health centers that remained from the 2001 war and the sanctions period were destroyed, medicines were not available, and medical equipment ceased to function for lack of spare parts and electricity. So the probability of Iraqi children dying reached three times the level of a comparable country, neighboring Jordan.

In the context of this widespread and growing despair, the U.S.

government began to establish a new regime in Iraq. The first move came quickly with the appointment of an interim team under a retired American general, Jay Garner, who had become a defense contractor and was known in the Middle East for his close ties to Israel; on May 24 he was replaced by L. Paul Bremer III, a former ambassador and current businessman who, in one of his first acts, ordered what was left of the Iraqi army to disperse. This probably was the single most important act of his administration, because the ragged, defeated, and dispirited men took with them—or looted on their way home—their arms. When they arrived at home, they found destruction everywhere. Many of their relatives and friends who had not been killed were wounded and lacked all chance of receiving medical care. No one had any money. Food was in such short supply that starvation was a clear and present danger. Everyone was desperate. Even those with essential jobs, like doctors, were not being paid. There was no public order as police, also unpaid, had drifted away. Whole cities were without firefighters. So driven by hunger or by greed, former soldiers formed gangs to protect what they had or to get what they desperately needed. Looting became just another form of shopping. Without orders to stop it, the American army merely observed the destruction. The damage everywhere was immense, and some of it, like the looting of Baghdad's great museum of antiquities, was an irreplaceable loss to world culture.*

Little or no preparation had been made to cope with this catastrophe. A State Department plan, the result of a year-long study by

* Milbry Polk and Angela M. H. Schuster, eds., *The Looting of the Iraq Museum, Baghdad: The Lost Legacy of Ancient Mesopotamia* (New York: Abrams, 2005).

the Future of Iraq Working Group, simply disappeared in the Pentagon and was not given to the military commanders or read by the incoming American administrators. The State Department official who had supervised the preparation of the study, Thomas Warrick, was blocked by the Defense Department from joining Bremer's administration in Baghdad, in which only one man, Ambassador Hume Horan, really knew Arabic or had a sophisticated understanding of Iraq. Indeed, no one had thought to brief senior military officers, so that many did not know the difference between a Kurd and an Arab, a Sunni and a Shii, a torturer (like the man the American administrators appointed to run the prison it had taken over at Abu Ghraib) or those he had tortured when he administered the prison for Saddam. Those Iraqis with whom the Americans were in touch were themselves out of touch with Iraqi society. Many had not been present in Iraq for decades. None put forth any competent advice on how to meet the urgent needs of hungry, crippled, or homeless people, and some of them were distrusted or even violently disliked by their fellow countrymen. It was not an auspicious beginning. And it got worse.

Spontaneously, without leaders, thousands of Iraqis took to the streets in what were at first peaceful demonstrations in Mosul, Fallujah, Baghdad, and other cities. Their demand was basic—food. But fearful, unprepared, and ill-informed American soldiers opened fire on them. In Fallujah, a city of about 350,000 people that came to epitomize the occupation, the killing of fifteen protesters in April 2003 by American soldiers triggered the first serious attack on American forces. That was the beginning of the Iraqi insurgency.

The American reaction was surprise. Why were the Iraqis attacking Americans? Surely they knew that the Americans had liberated them from the awful tyranny of Saddam and were trying their best to meet Iraqi needs. Their only explanation was that the attacks did not constitute a popular insurgency but were only the work of criminals and a few "Baathist remnants." Some of the protesters certainly were "remnants" of the old regime and some certainly were criminals, but small groups who were neither soon coalesced into larger organizations in response to the urgings of nationalism, and the looting of goods was replaced by attacks for political purposes. These attacks focused with increasing sophistication on targets that the insurgents obviously hoped would cause the Americans to leave. By the middle of the summer of 2003 some of these attacks were relatively massive—oil pipelines (which many Iraqis thought had been the object of the American invasion) were twice blown up in August. Those Iraqis who were thought to collaborate with the Americans were also attacked. Even the United Nations headquarters was blown up.

As the attacks became more systematic and widespread, blaming "Baathist remnants" no longer sufficed, and the search was on for foreign terrorists. When Secretary of State Powell visited Baghdad that September, he was told that up to two thousand foreign militants were operating there.* The American response was to fall back

* Experts on partisan warfare know that inserting even a few foreigners into any population anywhere is extremely difficult. Doing so requires organization, money, and long preparation, none of which the Iraqi insurgents had in 2003. Moreover, Iraq had enough angry people, with enough training and with access to weapons and explosives without foreign assistance, to explain the insurgency. While there were certainly some foreigners among the insurgents, the charge that they were its main force was a red herring. And later, in early June 2006, the killing of the best-known foreign insurgent, the Jordanian Abu Musab al-Zarqawi, did little or nothing even to slow down the insurgency.

on purely military action—at nearly the scale of shock and awe. By the end of 2003 ground troops were calling in air strikes using two-thousand-pound bombs and missiles for the first time since the Iraqi armed forces had surrendered in April. Such major weapons flattened the buildings in whole neighborhoods. These strikes were often followed by strafing by AC-130 Spectre gunships that inevitably wounded or killed large numbers of people. American troops also razed the houses and cut down trees along roads, both to make the laying of mines more difficult and to punish suspected supporters of the insurgents. Despite the charge from Amnesty International that the American tactics appeared to violate the Geneva Conventions, the commander of the 82nd Airborne Division, which was the lead element in the counterinsurgency, said, "This is war, and we're not going to prosecute the war holding one hand behind our back. When we identify positively an enemy target, we're going to go ahead and take it out with every means we have available." In reply, the insurgents employed such weapons as they had or could devise. They even used such "low-tech" delivery systems as donkey carts to fire rockets and assembled mines from an estimated three million tons of unexploded aircraft bombs and abandoned artillery shells. A new acronym entered the military patois, IED, for "improvised explosive device." These shells proved to be one of the most lethal weapons in the hands of the insurgents. Large numbers of the attacks were mounted by Sunni Muslims, but by June 2003 Shiis had joined in. Shia religious leaders privately warned the American authorities that while they appreciated the American overthrow of Saddam Hussein, an American presence in Iraq of more than a few months was not acceptable to their followers.

Fear of violent death was—and remains—uppermost in the minds of most Iraqis, at least those in the major cities, where the traditional protections afforded by clan and neighborhood are weakest. The American forces do not keep records of civilian deaths (as the American military commander said, "We don't do body counts"), and allegedly the Coalition Provisional Authority in December 2003 ordered the Iraqi Health Ministry to stop collecting statistics on civilian casualties. But two English organizations have attempted to do so. The highly respected English medical journal *The Lancet* conducted a nationwide survey based on a sample of 998 households in some 33 "clusters." Made under very difficult circumstances, the report was published in November 2004; it was widely criticized as exaggerated but was subjected to rigorous review before being published, and no more comprehensive survey has yet been made. It came to the conclusion that "the death toll associated with the invasion and occupation of Iraq is probably about 100,000 people, and may be much higher" and that "more than half the deaths reportedly caused by the occupying forces were women and children."

The second organization, known as Iraq Body Count, estimated civilian casualties by a different method: it counted casualties only when at least two media outlets reported them. So it acknowledged that the figures it published were less than the actual. But they are still appalling: from May 1, 2003, to April 30, 2004, it was 6,331; from May 1, 2004, to April 30, 2005, it was 11,312; and from May 1, 2005, to February 28, 2006, it was 12,617. These figures yield an average per diem of 20 in the first year, 31 in the second, and 36 in the third, then-still-incomplete, year.

Less dramatic are other causes of death and disease. One that will linger for decades or generations is use of depleted uranium metal shells for antitank warfare; such shells were used both in the 1991 war and in the 2003 invasion. Readings taken from Iraqi tanks destroyed by such shells show levels of radiation 2,500 times the normal, and radioactive debris from an estimated one thousand tons of depleted uranium is known to have been carried widely by wind-blown dust. Studies by medical specialists have indicated that following the 1991 conflict, large numbers of Iraqi children developed leukemia and various birth defects. Thousands more almost certainly will in the years to come.

A number of Iraqi cities have been virtually razed in counter-insurgency operations. One city, however, may be taken as the epitome of them all: Fallujah. Little about Fallujah formerly distinguished it from other Iraqi cities, but now a great deal does. It has been nearly destroyed. A visiting reporter, embedded with the American troops sent to suppress the insurgency there, described the city as a "tableau of destroyed buildings, burned-out cars, battered mosques, and piles of rubble." Perhaps 200,000 residents fled the city during the fighting. Those who remained were considered insurgents, and many were shot out of hand. Even a Red Crescent convoy with medicines was prevented from reaching the city hospital, which itself was declared off limits for the remaining wounded inhabitants.

So severe was the fighting that the American administrator Bremer thought further military action would cause a collapse in the negotiations that he had undertaken to choose an Iraqi interim governing council. But apparently the Marine commander at Fallujah pressed ahead anyway and also enrolled a former Baathist general to help subdue the city. Bremer said he thought the American military commander, General Ricardo Sanchez, who wanted to stop the assault at least temporarily, "had been blindsided by the Marine commander in Fallujah." If the situation at headquarters was confused, the situation on the ground was catastrophic. News reports indicate that much of the shooting was uncontrolled. One news report quoted a Marine sergeant as saying he saw his colleagues kill thirty civilians at one checkpoint in a single day. "We're committing genocide," he said. By December 2004 more than two hundred buildings had been leveled, and even the buried power lines had been so badly damaged that American engineers said they would have to be ripped out and replaced from scratch.

The weight of ordnance fired was extraordinary. Against what was apparently just sniper fire, a single Marine contingent fired thirty-five or more heavy artillery shells plus an estimated thirty thousand rounds from rifles and machine guns. Far more devastating than heavy shells and "light" ammunition were the internationally banned chemical weapons that the American forces used in what one Iraqi called "a grim reminder of Saddam Hussein's gassing of the Kurds in 1988." "Willy Pete," as the soldiers called white phosphorus, incinerates everyone within a radius of 150 meters, actually caramelizing the skin of the victims. White phosphorus is an internationally banned weapon. Although they first denied it, military spokesmen admitted that it was used, but, they said, only for illumination during the night. Documentary photos filmed by an Italian camera crew show a very different and hideous reality: some victims are still in their beds, with their bodies completely burned.* No one knows the number of civilian casualties, but they are believed to have been in the thousands. Attacking troops were told that the city was a "free fire zone" and that anyone, of any age or sex, was a target and should be shot. But the commanding American general said that he was not aware of any civilian casualties.

Survivors showed their anger to the rare journalist who ventured into the city embedded with the troops by uttering such remarks as "The Americans are the terrorists. They keep on killing Iraqi women and children . . . Death to the Americans." Another said, "We don't have any tanks. We don't have any jets . . . Our only weapon is the Koran." Iraqis are likely to remember Fallujah as Russians remember Stalingrad: an icon of the desperate struggle to repulse the invader. Surely the memory will fuel hatred of America for many years. Unbelievably, at least some Americans appeared to be oblivious to the pain they had caused. During one phase of the fighting the commander of the 82nd Airborne Division said, "We think we will see the day when we are playing soccer with them [the residents of Fallujah]. But it won't be in a few weeks."

Fallujah was not the only Iraqi city to be destroyed in the quest for security. Indeed, the list of destroyed settlements is long. Americans would do well to remember the bitter remark that the Roman historian Tacitus attributed to the leader of Rome's enemy, the insurgent Britons: the Romans, he said, "create a desolation and call it peace."

Peace or at least stability is always the casualty of guerrilla war,

---

* The documentary is called "Fallujah: The Hidden Massacre." Photographs can be viewed at www.informationclearinghouse.info/article10907.htm.

so of course Iraq has experienced a breakdown of public order. With an unemployment rate (depending on the area) estimated at between 30 and 50 percent—far beyond what any society can sustain—large numbers of Iraqis have become both desperate and unrestrained by the normal inhibitions. Consequently, although the prison population has soared to about sixteen thousand at the time of this writing, crime has risen to unprecedented heights. And given that virtually all Iraqis are armed, much of that crime is violent. As Amnesty International commented on March 9, 2006, "Not only has the Iraqi government failed to provide minimal protection for its citizens, it has pursued a policy of rounding up and torturing innocent men and women. Its failure to punish those who have committed torture has added to the breakdown of the rule of law."

Both the British administration in its time and the American administration today have provided Iraq with constitutions. The American-written interim constitution was approved on March 8, 2004, by the American-controlled Iraqi Governing Council. It had been secretly drafted by American lawyers with no Iraqi participation. Yet Secretary of State Powell lauded it as "a major achievement," and Prime Minister Blair called it "the foundation stone" of a democratic Iraq. Almost exactly eighty years before, in 1924, British officials had coached a group of carefully vetted Iraqis in taking an almost identical action. Just as Americans asserted in 2004, so the British had proclaimed in 1924 that the constitution was the harbinger of independence. Iraqis remembered, however, that directly or indirectly Britain continued to rule Iraq for the next thirty-four years. How long, Iraqis asked, would America actually rule their country?

One impression seems clear: when the Iraqi people think of Britain and the United States, they do not think of democracy; rather their minds burn with anger and grief over the destruction of their country by invading foreigners.

In *My Year in Iraq* Paul Bremer reported on his efforts to choose an Iraqi leader. He rejected the candidate offered by the UN mediator, the former foreign minister of Algeria, Lakhdar Brahimi. Brahimi wanted Bremer to choose an American-trained nuclear scientist who had been imprisoned by Saddam Hussein for eleven years from 1979 for refusing to cooperate in Saddam's secret weapons program. Hussein al-Shahristani had escaped from prison in 1991 and spent some years abroad working against Saddam. When he returned to Iraq after the invasion in 2003, he set up a private charity to help families harmed by the war. So Brahimi found him a very attractive candidate, but like the leading Shia religious leader, Shahristani had refused to meet with the officials of the Coalition Provisional Authority. When Bremer reported this to President Bush, as Mr. Bremer wrote, "the president went straight to the heart of the matter as he saw it: 'It's important to have someone who's willing to stand up and thank the American people for their sacrifice in liberating Iraq. I don't expect us to pick a yes man. But at least I want someone who will be grateful. . . . We've got to be certain the new PM won't ask us to leave the day after sovereignty.' " Bremer reminded the president, Powell, Rumsfeld, and Rice "how deeply unpopular the Coalition had become under the incessant barrage of Arab propaganda and mounting security concerns. Perhaps the end of the formal occupation would help bring greater acceptance of the need for Coalition troops." Bush was unmoved. Al-Shahristani was passed over. Then, despite Brahimi's opposition to him for his long relationship with the CIA, Bremer appointed Iyad al-Allawi, who promised to emphasize "security" as his priority.

At this time, Easter 2004, President Bush gave a radio address in which he condemned "a small faction attempting to derail Iraqi democracy and seize power." The phrase "a small faction" clearly stuck in Bremer's throat. At that time, as he wrote, "the broader security situation continued to deteriorate. Insurgents mounted attacks on the oil pipelines, denying the government petroleum revenues. Our military convoys were being struck so regularly that on April 17 it looked as if I would have to order food rationing at the CPA. There was a big jump in attacks in the Sunni-dominated western Baghdad suburb of Abu Ghraib, and intelligence reports suggested plans for major uprisings in other Sunni cities such as Baiji, Tikrit, and Mosul." It was obviously difficult to reconcile the president's war with Bremer's.

Meanwhile, the condition of the Iraqi people continued to deteriorate. A *Washington Post* correspondent reported in November 2004 that "acute malnutrition among young children, already severe during the sanctions regime, has nearly doubled since the United States led an invasion of the country 20 months ago; it is now far higher than rates in Haiti." The article pointed out that 60 percent of rural residents and 20 percent of urban dwellers had access only to contaminated water and that the sewer systems were still in disarray. Residents, he said, commented that Saddam's government restored electricity within two months after the 1991 war ended, but, as he quoted the Iraqi planning minister, "although a large percentage in Iraq is connected to water, electricity and sewage networks, the supply is too unstable to make a difference to their lives." In fact, about seven in every ten Iraqis still were unable to get clean drinking and bathing water. Many of the three in ten Iraqis who did had to walk to sources that were about a quarter of an hour away to fill cans and carry them back. With electricity working only a few hours a day, sewage treatment, refrigeration, and cooling—almost necessities in areas where summer heat rises to over 120° F (50° C)—also broke down. Since factories and other businesses were able to work only part time if at all and consequently did not hire workers, unemployment averaged 40 percent with some areas rising to 50 percent. As the Iraqi minister of electric power said, "When you lose electricity, the country is destroyed."

Production of electricity depended primarily on oil. Production was down and going lower. In December 2005 and January 2006 it had fallen from the prewar average of 2.5 million barrels a day to less than half, around 1.1 million barrels. The problem was not simply that production was down and unlikely to rise significantly in the foreseeable future (ten years was a common prediction) but that poorly maintained oil fields suffer long-term damage resulting from the way the fields have been exploited, which results in a smaller portion of the reserve being ultimately recoverable. Thus Iraq was losing not only current revenues but the assets on which its long-term future will depend.

The American answer was to bring in British and American oil companies. Negotiations with them had begun in Washington even before the invasion. They continued in Baghdad by the CPA well before Iraqi "sovereignty" had been granted. In return for long-term (twenty-five or even forty-year), highly favorable contracts known as "production sharing agreements," the American and British companies would provide the capital to restart Iraqi oil production. On the surface, that seemed a workmanlike and even advantageous solution, at least to the American authorities. But as independent international experts have pointed out,* such agreements are likely to cost Iraq over the terms of the contracts upward of $200 billion in lost revenues. To most Iraqis and indeed many foreigners, the move to turn over Iraq's oil reserves to American and British companies seemed confirmation that the real purpose of the invasion was to secure for Americans Iraq's rich, lightweight, and inexpensively produced oil. For further confirmation, they point to the fact that the only government building that was adequately protected by American soldiers during their attack and initial occupation from looting in 2003 was the Oil Ministry, which housed the detailed geological studies of the Iraqi fields.

There are signs that the U.S. military has become almost desperate and that, despite attempts to engage in civic action programs that were inspired by the Vietnam War experience, it is being driven to do what all armies are designed to do: employ force. As we write, American forces have returned to mounting massive military actions involving thousands of troops, tanks, and aircraft against areas suspected of housing insurgents. They have also made what Iraqis see as

* Greg Muttitt, "Crude Designs: The Rip-Off of Iraq's Oil Wealth," *Platform* and other contributing groups, November 2005; also see Philip Thornton, "Iraq's Oil: The Spoils of War," *Independent,* November 22, 2005. Their findings were confirmed to William R. Polk by Adib al Jadir, who was Iraq's minister of economy, minister of industry, and then chairman and president of the Iraq National Oil Company.

attacks on their culture and religion, as in the March 28, 2006, attack on a Baghdad Shia mosque where thirty-seven worshippers were killed during the evening prayer. As the Iraqi interior minister, a Shii who after all is an American appointee, commented on TV, "Entering the mosque and killing worshippers was a horrible violation." Another Iraqi government minister predicted, "I think we are going to have a firm stance against American forces because of this crime." The television station on which he spoke showed pictures throughout the night of bodies lying in pools of blood on the mosque floor. There are growing signs that these actions are producing antagonism that permeate a widening range of the society not only among the Sunni Arabs but also among the American-favored Shiis.

In his reflections on the 1991 Gulf War, former President Bush explained why he had not approved the policy that was later adopted by his son: "Had we gone the invasion route, the United States could conceivably still be an occupying power in a bitterly hostile land."* That is precisely what has happened. Even Richard Perle, one of the prime architects of the American invasion and the overthrow of Saddam, confessed in a recent debate with the Democratic National Committee chairman Howard Dean that the subsequent American military occupation of Iraq was "probably a mistake." Zalmay Khalilzad, the American ambassador to Iraq and one of the leading neoconservative advocates of the American invasion, admitted to a reporter from the *Los Angeles Times* on March 8, 2006, that "we have opened the Pandora's box, and the question is, what is the way forward?"

---

* *A World Transformed* (New York: Vintage, 1998), the book Bush and General Brent Scowcroft wrote on the war.

CHAPTER 4

Damage Report: The Impact on America of the Iraq War

THE IRAQ WAR has already lasted more than twice as long as the American involvement in what our grandfathers used to call the Great War. Fewer Americans have been involved in the Iraq war than in the First or Second World War or in the Korean or Vietnam wars, or in the bloodiest of all our wars, the Civil War of the 1860s, in which 600,000 young Americans killed one another. However, as will become clear, in many ways the conflict in faraway Iraq has been one of the most traumatic in the American experience.

When Americans were about to be sent to fight in Iraq, polls indicated that few of the young men and women even knew where it was. In fact, nationwide only about one in seven Americans between the ages of eighteen and twenty-four, those who would be most affected, could locate Iraq on a world map. Practically none of them knew what language was spoken there, what religion or religions were practiced, or how Iraqi society functioned. As has been said, "War is God's way of teaching Americans geography," but Americans have proven to be poor pupils. Even after three years of war in

Iraq, a Roper poll conducted in 2006 for *The National Geographic* found that six out of ten young Americans were still unable to locate it on a map. American ignorance about Iraq played an important part in the young soldiers' hostile reaction to Iraqis and in their disillusionment with the results of their sacrifice.

Surprising to many overseas observers of American society is the fact that, despite our own diverse origins, we have little sympathy for or rapport with other people. To generation after generation of American soldiers sent abroad, foreigners were "geesers" (during the Mexican War), "gugus" or "niggers" (during the Philippine insurrection), "krauts" or "wops" (during World War II), "slopes" or "gooks" (during the Vietnam War), and now in Iraq "ragheads," "hajis," and "sand niggers." Racism is always close to the surface in American society and comes boiling up in times of conflict.

Ignorance among the soldiers was echoed at the highest levels of the American government. Although a State Department task force prepared a detailed multivolume study to guide administrators of Iraq after the invasion, none of the senior officials read it until well into the occupation. As Paul Bremer writes in his account of his time in Baghdad, he did not even know that such a study had been made until he read about it in the press after he got to Baghdad, but he "eventually had a chance to read the fifteen-volume study." In their contacts with senior officials of the American government, the British—old hands at administering conquered Asian territories—were astonished at how little preparation the American government had made for what would obviously be a "protracted and costly" occupation. This lack of preparation would shape the American occupation and explain in part why the Bush administration was unable to cope with the crisis it had created.

The crisis has a number of facets, but the most graphic and tragic in its impact on Americans has been the American casualties. No one in either the civilian or the military parts of the American government was prepared for them: during the invasion, which relied upon aerial attacks to "soften" the Iraqi army and then on massive deployment of armor to crush those formations that remained intact, American casualties had been minimal. The war seemed to have been won "on the cheap." Militarily there was no contest. But the American high command neglected what students of warfare have long known: that there is a vast difference between winning battles and winning a war. As in Vietnam, even though battles had been won over the broken and demoralized army, the war would enter a second phase, during which American casualties would far exceed what the military had experienced during the battle phase. Deaths in the battle phase and the occupation as of July 29, 2006, reached 2,578, and many times that number have been seriously wounded or crippled.

That the number of casualties has not been larger is due to one of the striking features of modern warfare: the deployment of technically sophisticated medical support for the troops. Almost within minutes of an engagement, the wounded are either treated on the spot or evacuated to a hospital. Certainly many of the 17,381 (as of this writing) wounded American soldiers who would have died in previous wars were saved. That is the good news. The bad news is that roughly half these men and women were so severely wounded that they face a lifelong struggle to cope with their disabilities. As Stephan Fihn of the Department of Veterans Affairs told *USA Today* reporter William M. Welch, the severity of their wounds is often worse than in previous wars because of the nature of urban guerrilla warfare. The biggest difference today, he said, "is the incidence of multiple amputations from bomb blasts, as opposed to the bullet or fragment wounds to the chest or stomach, more common in previous wars. The blasts have also left some soldiers with significant brain trauma." The latter, the result of concussion, was not predicted and indeed not recorded until three years after the invasion. Brain trauma is now predicted to affect upward of fifty thousand men and women.

One problem with such statistics is that they are inevitably incomplete. Not all the deaths or wounds show up at the time the statistics are compiled. Two sources of casualties particularly stand out and will cause damage to individual Americans, their families, and American society as a whole far into the future. The first is the use of depleted uranium in antiarmor shells. We have pointed out that they had a tragic effect on Iraqi children, but they also affected American soldiers. Their use is a controversial and little-noted aspect of both the 1991 Gulf War and the 2003 invasion of Iraq. These weapons continue to give off radiation for many years after being employed. Those who handle them risk experiencing the effects of radiation; depleted uranium may be at least partly responsible for Gulf War Syndrome. And because radiated particles are broadcast by winds in the vast dust storms of Iraq, practically all the American soldiers were exposed. Thus, although it is not often discussed, some 169,000 of the 580,400 soldiers who took part in the 1991 Gulf War were on permanent medical disability a decade later. Many veterans had developed cancer. Again controversial and as yet little studied is the charge that men affected by radiation from depleted uranium during the 1991 Gulf War can transmit their afflictions to others. Competent medical authorities assert that men exposed to high levels of radiation from depleted uranium can harm their sexual partners, forcing them to have hysterectomies, and can perhaps cause birth defects in their children. Hundreds of tons of these weapons were employed in both Iraq wars. At the very least, the long-term effects are likely to be painful and serious for tens or hundreds of thousands of young Americans. Already some soldiers are developing cancer from the 2003 invasion of Iraq. As presidential adviser General Brent Scowcroft commented after the 1991 Gulf War, "Depleted uranium is more of a problem than we thought when it was developed."

As though physical damage were not enough, the Iraq wars have been extraordinary in their impact on the mental health of American soldiers. The surgeon general's December 2005 report, published in the *Journal of the American Medical Association*, estimated that more than one in three soldiers and Marines who had served in Iraq during the 2003 invasion and the subsequent occupation sought mental health treatment. According to a restricted Department of Defense survey, nearly two thousand who applied for help were worried that they were likely to inflict wounds on themselves or to contemplate suicide, while ten times that many suffered frequent nightmares about what they had done or been exposed to. And some 3,700 feared that they would lose control and hurt others. The report points out that "Iraq veterans are far more likely to have witnessed people getting wounded or killed" than veterans of other wars. So many men and women fall in this category that they have overwhelmed the medical system; consequently, nearly two-thirds of Iraq veterans who screened positive for post-traumatic stress disorder (PTSD) and other psychiatric disorders are not receiving treatment. Even the limited number of former combatants who are getting treatment cost the Department of Veterans Affairs $3.2 billion a year. What impact their disabilities will have on their ability to hold jobs, raise families, or even live within communities cannot as yet be predicted. Their large number, however, suggests that disability is one of the major unseen costs of the Iraq war. In 2005 at least fifty thousand returning veterans were found to be in need of psychiatric care. Others may have been affected in ways that are not yet evident.

Every war has a home front. But as far as we have been able to determine, there is no study yet available on the impact on families of the deaths of more than 2,500 young men and women, the severe or crippling wounding of another 8,000, the long-term effects of Gulf War Syndrome and/or cancer of untold thousands, or the impaired mental health of scores of thousands more. These traumas radiate out into the community at large. At least a thousand children have already been deprived of a parent, and a far larger number of families have been—or will be—afflicted.

Less painful than the personal costs are the monetary costs on the society as a whole. Curiously, these are almost as difficult to determine with any accuracy as the health impairments. Some have reported that, having gotten its allies to contribute, America made a "small profit" on the 1991 Gulf War, but this is untrue. In order to get the allies to contribute or even to support the war effort, America had to pay out (or forgo debts in the amount of) tens of billions of dollars for Egypt, Turkey, and Syria as well as get Saudi Arabia and the Gulf states to subsidize the Soviet Union. As William Nordhaus pointed out in the December 2002 issue of *Foreign Affairs*, measured in 2002 dollars the first Gulf War cost the United States roughly $80 billion.

A RAND Corporation study estimated that the interwar period cost the United States between $30 and $60 billion *yearly*—for a total of $300–$600 billion. Even this amount is probably an understatement. For the 2003 invasion and the subsequent occupation the allocated outlay—which is only a *part* of the real costs—was in the hundreds of billions of dollars and has grown at roughly 20 percent yearly; it is now at about $7.1 billion a month or $237 million a day. Taking those astronomical figures down closer to earth means that the occupation of Iraq costs roughly $10 million each hour.

The most recent and most sophisticated analysis of the costs of the Iraq war and the occupation has been prepared by Linda Bilmes and Joseph Stiglitz.* The authors believe that their "estimates are very conservative, and it could be that the final costs will be much higher. And it should be noted that they do not include the costs of the conflict to either Iraq or the UK." Bilmes and Stiglitz used standard economic and accounting/budgetary methods rather than just the sums allocated by Congress. Thus they took into account "lifetime healthcare and disability payments to returning veterans, replenishment of military hardware, and increased recruitment costs." They also took into account "the social costs of the resources deployed (e.g., reserve pay is less than the opportunity wage and disability pay is less than forgone earnings)" and estimated the effects of the war on the overall performance of the economy. As they wrote,

* National Bureau of Economic Research, Working Paper 12054, available online at www.nber.org/papers/w12054. Bilmes is a well-known authority on the budget and former assistant secretary of commerce who now teaches at the John F. Kennedy School of Government at Harvard. Stiglitz, who won the Nobel Prize in economics in 2001, teaches at Columbia University.

"Even taking a conservative approach and assuming all US troops return by 2010, we believe the true costs exceed a trillion dollars. Using the CBO [Congressional Budget Office] projection of maintaining troops in Iraq through 2015, the true costs may exceed $2 trillion." That is *over thirty times* the estimate that Secretary of Defense Rumsfeld made on behalf of the Bush administration.

As staggering as this figure is, it does not take into account either the depleted uranium health issue or the increased price of oil in recent months. Bilmes and Stiglitz had noted that oil went "from $25 a barrel before the war to around $50 today." It was on the $50 figure that they based a part of their calculations. Oil has since increased, at the time of this writing, about 60 percent to $80 a barrel. In a separate article, "Waging the Trillion-dollar War," Bilmes estimated that each five-dollar increase in the price of oil reduces our national income by about $17 billion a year. With oil today at $30 more than the figure she and Stiglitz used, our national income will be reduced by about $102 billion.

The Bilmes-Stiglitz study pointed out that the authors "have not been able to quantify many of what may turn out to be the most important costs of the Iraq venture." We now will attempt to address some of these costs. We will deal first with those that directly affect America domestically, and then address those that affect America's position in the world.

As the former secretary of commerce in the Nixon administration, Peter Peterson, has calculated, "Just keeping two divisions engaged in 'stability operations' in Iraq for one week costs $1 billion; keeping them engaged for a full year would cost the entire GDP [gross domestic product] of New Zealand." Aware that Americans are loath to pay these costs and eager to ease the economic pain of the war, the Bush administration has cut domestic taxes while borrowing huge amounts of money abroad. As James K. Galbraith of the Lyndon B. Johnson School of Public Affairs of the University of Texas commented, "The fact is, we are acquiring an empire. But the men in charge do not want to pay for it. . . . The problem of empires, historically, is not military defeat. It is bankruptcy." In 2004 the United States borrowed about $540 billion. So far this huge amount of borrowing has disguised from American consumers, at least in part, the growing cost of the war. But as the economist Paul Krugman has written, it has placed on America a burden that our children and grandchildren will have to assume. Krugman believes that while "President Bush has excoriated the 'death tax,' as he calls the estate tax . . . his profligacy will leave every American child facing a 'birth tax' of about $150,000. That's right: every American child arrives owing that much, partly to babies in China and Japan. No wonder babies cry."

The costs go beyond the monetary: they include cuts in federal expenditures for social services, environmental protection, education, health care, even research on alternative sources of energy, cleaning up nuclear waste, rehabilitation of cities and highways, preservation of public parks, and many of the other things that affect the "good life" sought by all Americans. Critics of the administration believe that these cuts were made on ideological rather than budgetary grounds, but the budget gives a sense of what could have been done with some of the money spent on the war.

Not only has the physical quality of life been affected; the moral effects of the war are just beginning to come into focus. To put it simply, all war is brutalizing both to the strong (us) and to the weak (the

Iraqis), and guerrilla warfare is particularly degrading. Horrified by what the Vietnam War was doing to American society, Martin Luther King, Jr., warned, "It should be incandescently clear that no one who has any concern for the integrity and life of America today can ignore the present war. If America's soul becomes totally poisoned, part of the autopsy must read Vietnam."

Was the Vietnam War just an aberration? There is ample evidence that it was not. Most Americans remember Vietnam, but none recall America's first real experience with guerrilla warfare, the 1899–1900 Philippine insurrection. It had all the elements that we attribute to Vietnam: American soldiers destroyed dozens of villages and routinely tortured prisoners. The favorite torture, sounding a very modern note, was the "water cure" in which water was forced down a captive's throat and then forced out by men kneeling on his stomach. Again in a modern echo, senior U.S. commanders in the Philippines tried hard to prevent news of these atrocities and casualties from reaching the American public. The commanding American general personally altered the dispatches sent out by journalists. His chief censor told the outraged reporters, "My instructions are to shut off everything that could hurt [President William] McKinley's administration," and when the reporters confronted General Elwell S. Otis, "he did not deny suppressing the facts. He had to do it, he insisted, to shield the [American] people from distortions and sensationalism." So what they had themselves witnessed, "such as American soldiers bayoneting wounded *amigos* [insurgents], the looting of homes and churches, and so on," was not to be reported.*

---

* Leon Wolff, *Little Brown Brother: America's Forgotten Bid for Empire Which Cost 250,000 Lives* (London: Longmans, Green, 1961), 261.

By 1900, America had almost the same number of troops, 150,000, in the Philippines as we have today in Iraq. As President Bush did on May 1, 2003, the American commander then announced that the war was over—the mission was accomplished. There "will be no more real fighting . . . [just] little skirmishes which amount to nothing." But as the historian Leon Wolff wryly commented, "Two years and six thousand U.S. casualties later" there had been over a thousand separate "engagements" in the Philippines.

As was already evident in the Philippines campaign, warfare between insurgents or guerrillas and regular troops inevitably lowers the moral standards of both. In Vietnam far more happened than the few publicized massacres like the one at My Lai. Soldiers' tales of the horror of combat have begun to come out. In one, as the Associated Press reported on October 20, 2003, "an elite unit of American soldiers mutilated and killed hundreds of unarmed villagers over seven months in 1967 during the Vietnam War, and a U.S. Army investigation was closed with no charges filed . . . Soldiers of the Tiger Force unit of the army's 101st Airborne Division dropped grenades into bunkers where villagers—including women and children—were hiding . . . Soldiers told *The* [Toledo] *Blade* they severed ears from the dead and strung them on shoelaces to wear around their necks . . . William Doyle, a former Tiger Force sergeant now living in Willow Springs, Missouri, said he killed so many civilians in 1967 that he lost count." The soldiers recalled that officers knew what they were doing and in some cases even encouraged them.

"My son-in-law, a young man of impeccable integrity who fought with the Third Marine Division near Da Nang, tells us of the shocking, barbarous behavior that he witnessed in Vietnam," reports George McGovern, who visited the war zones three times while a

U.S. senator. After an army investigation, "the only soldier to be officially punished was a sergeant who had triggered the investigation by reporting that a member of the Tiger Force had decapitated an infant. (He was reprimanded, as *The New Yorker* discovered, for stating that he had witnessed the incident when in fact he had learned of it from others.)" It is sobering to find that American troops are now under investigation for atrocities in several Iraqi towns. Haditha, where even three-year-old children and an old man in a wheelchair were murdered along with many others in a daylong rampage, may be the My Lai of the Iraq war.

Fear and anger at least partially explain, even if they do not justify, atrocities committed in combat, but the ghastly treatment of bound and hooded prisoners cannot be so explained. The Bush administration has invented a new category to justify extralegal treatment—"unlawful enemy combatants"—thus placing them outside the requirements of the Geneva Conventions on warfare agreed to by the United States and reaffirmed by the Bush administration. President Bush stated in November 2005, "We do not torture." Secretary of Defense Rumsfeld said that "the prisoners in Guantánamo Bay are being treated humanely. The idea that there's any policy of abuse or policy of torture is false, flat false." Perhaps Rumsfeld misunderstood the meaning of torture. His and the administration's definition of torture, an English High Court judge commented on February 16, 2006, "does not appear to coincide with that of most civilized nations."

For years it was impossible to check U.S. government statements denying torture. Now, we know what observers have seen and prisoners have reported in the nearly one hundred prisons that the

United States maintains, in which more than forty thousand Iraqis have been incarcerated since March 2003. Although its access was limited—and in June 2006 was even further restricted—Amnesty International was able to document some cases and found that the bodies of some of the prisoners who had died in custody "bore injuries consistent with torture." The International Committee of the Red Cross had more access but is prohibited by its own rules from disclosing what it found, Ironically, the reply of the military authorities at Guantánamo to "concerns" expressed by the Red Cross constitutes a virtual condemnation of the military authorities' own practices.*

Why would prison guards torture prisoners? There are several possible answers. The first is anger. When a guard hears of other soldiers killed or even mutilated by an enemy whom he cannot understand and whose motives appear evil to him, he may lose inhibitions that would otherwise prevent him from committing sadistic acts. The second answer is that, as the English philosopher Lord Acton observed, "Power tends to corrupt, and absolute power corrupts absolutely." Acton was thinking of political power, but even more formative of human action is the dominance given to jailers over prisoners and soldiers over civilians. It seems to be a characteristic of the human species that the sight of weakness provokes violence. Third, we are all to some degree disciplined, even formed, by society, and for soldiers in a strange land, the army is society. Its rules are their law, and its mores are their standards. So what soldiers perceive as the

---

* Staff Judge Advocate to "File," January 24, 2002, Department of Defense, United States Southern Command, Joint Task Force 160.

conduct desired by the army governs how most will act. Thus it is crucial to see what the army appeared to want. One answer is given in a *Washington Post* editorial of November 22, 2004. "Investigations have determined," the *Post* editors wrote, "that some U.S. interrogators who tortured detainees at the Abu Ghraib prison reasonably believe that their actions had been authorized by a memorandum from the headquarters of Lieutenant General Richard S. Sanchez . . . although those methods clearly violate the Geneva conventions. They were sanctioned by Gen. Sanchez's legal staff 'using reasoning from the president's memorandum of February 7, 2002,' which determined that the conventions could be set aside for people deemed 'unlawful combatants.' " Specifically and in detail, Secretary of Defense Rumsfeld gave formal approval for the use of "hooding," "exploitation of phobias" (such as fear of dogs), "stress positions" (that is sitting, standing, or hanging in painful positions for long periods of time), and "deprivation of light and auditory stimuli." These and other "coercive tactics [are] ordinarily forbidden by the Army Field Manual. (However, he reserved judgment on other methods including 'waterboarding,' a form of simulated drowning.)" In short, as Jane Mayer commented, "whatever its intent, what Rumsfeld's memo permitted was 'torture.' "* In August 2002, based on this decision at the highest level of the administration, the Office of the Legal Counsel of the U.S. Department of Justice issued a memorandum secretly authorizing the CIA "to inflict pain and suffering on detainees during interrogation up to the level caused by 'organ failure.' " Then on April 16, 2003, "24 harsh techniques" were approved, and

* "The Memo," *The New Yorker,* February 27, 2006.

"Rumsfeld's signature gave it the weight of a military order." As Mayer reported, "This document, now widely known as the Torture Memo, which [David] Addington [special assistant to Vice President Cheney] helped to draft," and others were "leaked to the press in 2004 after the Abu Ghraib scandal broke."

Before the scandal broke, some lower-ranking soldiers who were involved in torture stupidly took pictures of one another performing various obscene and vicious acts. The U.S. Army's criminal investigation division gathered 1,325 photographs, 93 video clips, 546 photographs of suspected dead Iraqi detainees, 660 images of adult pornography, and 29 pictures of U.S. troops engaged in simulated sex acts. Other pictures show blood-streaked cells and the battered face of a corpse packed in ice. These materials relate just to the months between October 18 and December 30, 2003, in the one prison of Abu Ghraib. They were leaked to the American online magazine Salon.com. These and other materials formed the basis for a small number of courts-martial and, under court order, have been authenticated by the Department of Justice, but as former director of the CIA Admiral Stansfield Turner commented on March 8, 2006, in the *Washington Post*, "Last August a four-star general was fired for having had an extramarital affair. Yet the day before, a Pentagon spokesman gave a limp explanation for why no two-, three- or four-star officer had been reprimanded for the prisoner abuse at Abu Ghraib . . . The buck for such errors stops at the Oval Office . . . Much is at stake in this failure to hold someone at an appropriate level accountable for what were grievous and disgraceful performances in these prisons."

The trial of Sergeant Michael J. Smith, who was convicted on

March 21, 2006, for using an attack dog in interrogation, shows that no attention was paid to the admonition of Admiral Turner. Sergeant Smith "said he was merely following interrogation procedures approved by the chief intelligence officer at Abu Ghraib, Col. Thomas M. Pappas. In turn, Colonel Pappas had said he had been following guidance from Maj. Gen. Geoffrey D. Miller, commander of the military prison at Guantánamo Bay, Cuba, who in September 2003 visited Iraq to discuss ways to 'set the conditions' for enhancing prison interrogations, as well as from superiors in Baghdad." But at Sergeant Smith's trial, General Miller was never called to testify. Smith faced a maximum sentence of eight and a half years but received only 179 days in prison. The punishment was regarded as a "slap on the wrist." Questioned by *New York Times* reporter Eric Schmitt, an army spokesman said that "more than 600 accusations of detainee abuse in Iraq and Afghanistan since October 2001 had been investigated, and that 251 officers and enlisted soldiers had been punished in some way for misconduct related to prisoners." The highest-ranking man was a captain. At this writing, one higher-ranking officer, Lieutenant Colonel Steven Jordan, faces seven formal charges for prisoner abuse.

An American lawyer, Thomas Wilner, who is a partner at the prestigious firm of Shearman & Sterling, which agreed to represent six Kuwaiti prisoners, spent two and a half years just trying to get access to his clients at Guantánamo. When permission was finally granted, he visited the prison eleven times, so he should have had a reasonably comprehensive view of conditions there. He reported in the *Los Angeles Times* of February 26, 2006, conditions that sound like they were lifted from accounts of Soviet torture under Stalin in

Arthur Koestler's *Darkness at Noon* and the horrible prison conditions described in Aleksandr Solzhenitsyn's *Gulag Archipelago.* Some
were worse: they were like medieval dungeons. Prisoners had become
virtually "nonpersons," out of touch with family and indeed the
whole world for years, questioned hundreds of times, charged with
no crime, confined in dark cells and so unable even to see the sun for
months on end, often hooded with legs shackled to the floor or, when
being moved, with legs shackled together, beaten or forced into
painful positions, terrified by attack dogs, and often threatened with
execution. Under these conditions, at least thirty-nine prisoners were
driven to attempt suicide—one prisoner is known to have tried ten
times even by slashing his throat with the only tool he could find, a
dull stick—and a number have gone on hunger strikes, after which
they were force-fed by tubes pushed up their noses. Wilner's client
lost one-third of his body weight, and on one occasion when Wilner
saw him, drops of blood dripped from his nose. Prison authorities refused Wilmer's request that his client be hospitalized. In June 2006
three prisoners at Guantánamo committed suicide.

Reviewing the growing evidence of American torture, Ray Mc-
Govern, a senior CIA officer who retired after twenty-seven years of
service and now works for the Church of the Savior, wrote to the
chairman of the House Committee on Intelligence to say that he was
returning the medal he had received from the CIA for "especially
commendable service" because of the issue of "torture, which inhab-
its the same category as rape and slavery—intrinsically evil. I do not
wish to be associated, however remotely, with an agency engaged in
torture."

If one is prepared to accept the Bush administration's distinction between "unlawful enemy combatants" and prisoners of war, which in terms of the Geneva Conventions is dubious at best, then consider the case of a man who clearly *was* a prisoner of war, Major General Abdul Hamid Mawhoush. Learning that his four sons had been arrested, Mawhoush presented himself at Forward Operating Base Tiger in western Iraq to find out why and to seek their release. He was then arrested himself. As the subsequent U.S. military investigation determined, he was "beaten repeatedly by various uniformed and non-military personnel. He was slapped, kicked, and beaten with sticks and hard rubber tubing. On the morning of 26 November [2003] General Mawhoush was stuffed head-first into a sleeping bag, which was then bound with inch-thick electrical cord." According to the testimony, the soldier who had overseen Mawhoush's interrogation, Chief Warrant Officer Lewis Welshofer, sat on his prisoner's chest while asking questions about his role in the burgeoning insurgency.

By his own admission, "Welshofer clamped his hand several times over his captive's mouth through the sleeping bag. He said he did this to prevent the general invoking the name of Allah. After about half an hour, Welshofer noticed that the general was not moving. He then opened the sleeping bag. When he saw what he thought was a sort of smile on the general's face, he thought Mawhoush was 'messing' with him, and he poured water on his face . . . General Mawhoush was dead." Autopsy photos showed at least forty-seven deep purple contusions all over Mawhoush's body.

Those of us who remember the Second World War will recall that none of the senior officers of the Germans, Italians, or Japanese were treated in this manner. The fact that the Axis armies occasionally tortured American prisoners was regarded as a sign of barbarity, indeed as a war crime, for which, when opportunity afforded, they would receive condign punishment. The court-martial ruled that Welshofer was not guilty of murder.

In Iraq, prisons are not the only locales where grievous cases of violence and murder have occurred. Indeed, the events that have occurred *outside* prisons are the most disturbing of all, because they involve what might be termed "casual" disregard for other human beings and are done by "normal" young men and women who are not interrogators or jailers. Consider just one of what may have been thousands of episodes of such violence. A young religion student from Florida who had been inducted into the army told *New York Times* columnist Bob Herbert, "Guys in my unit, particularly the younger guys, would drive by in their Humvee and shatter bottles over the heads of Iraqi civilians passing by. They'd keep a bunch of empty Coke bottles in the Humvee to break over people's heads." The young soldier said he had also witnessed incidents in which an army sergeant lashed a group of children with a steel Humvee antenna, and a Marine corporal planted a vicious kick in the chest of a six-year-old child. Later Herbert's informant was assigned to the Abu Ghraib prison where, he said, the violence could only be described as "sickening . . . Some inmates were beaten nearly to death." Among the more than 4,400 American troops who have gone AWOL, at least some must have shared the feelings of this young theology student.*

---

* Suzanne Goldenberg, "Woman Soldier Refuses to Return to Iraq, Claiming Sexual Harassment," *Guardian*, June 21, 2006.

It would be comforting to be told that these were isolated incidents, but they were not. The English medical journal *The Lancet*
published a survey of Iraq in November 2004 claiming that about
one in every seven U.S. soldiers and nearly one in every four Marines
had killed an Iraqi civilian. Shooting of wounded prisoners allegedly
has been common. The filming of one such incident by a Marine
during the siege of Fallujah shocked many Americans, but it did not
lead to a court-martial since, as the Marine Corps statement said,
"The corporal reasonably believed that the [wounded and unarmed
Iraqi, shown lying on the ground with his arms raised in supplica-
tion] posed a hostile threat to him and his fellow Marines." More recently, in June and July 2006, five cases alleging severe brutality, rape,
and murder have been filed by the U.S. Marine Corps, the U.S.
Army, or the FBI.

■   ■   ■

Of course, young Americans are no more vicious or cruel than any
other people, so their actions must be determined by the context
in which they have been put and the guidance they believe they
have received from their superiors. Taking them out of their own
society, where laws are enforced and social norms emphasize respect for other people, and thrusting them into a confrontation
with people whose language, culture, and politics they do not understand and who hate them for being there is surely a recipe to bring
out the worst in them. The history of guerrilla warfare demonstrates
this dehumanizing tendency among peoples of all religions and cul-
tures. It also demonstrates that the longer these conditions persist,

the greater the destruction of the values of the young men or women who are so placed. Ultimately a whole generation can lose its civic moorings.

Such damage is very hard to repair. Even returning to "normal" life becomes problematic; the demobilized soldier is apt to take home with him what he has learned. This experience should be a great warning of danger for the most cherished values of American society. Alarmingly, in the midst of the tragedy of the Iraq war, officials of the American government are already discussing how to fight future wars, and some of the administration's most senior advisers are advocating what amounts to perpetual war. Such officials need to hear again the grim verdict of General Sherman: "War is hell." They might also contemplate the observation of the eighteenth-century British conservative parliamentarian Edmund Burke: "A conscientious man would be cautious how he dealt with blood." It is worth noting that many of the loudest advocates of war are theoreticians who have never been near a battle.

All war is brutal, but insurgencies and counterinsurgencies are particularly frightening because they nearly always cause the participants to drop even modest attempts to keep warfare within some reasonable boundaries of law and decency. Americans have now seen this occur in three of our wars: the suppression of the Philippine nationalist rebellion in 1900, the Vietnam War of the 1960s, and the Iraq occupation today. In each of these conflicts American troops and intelligence officers engaged in activities that not only created great hatred of America but also corrupted the values for which we proclaimed we were fighting. Those were major episodes, but in between them, in our quest for "security," we sometimes allied ourselves with a collection of corrupt tyrannies and helped their security services learn the techniques of torture that would provoke such outrage later in Iraq.*

Torture has been the single most widely publicized aspect of the American occupation of Iraq, and it has done more to besmirch the reputation of America throughout the world than any other single set of actions. So shameful have been our practices at the prisons in Iraq that they were withheld from the public as long as possible. When they finally became known, investigations substantiated the worst of the charges. But the only persons so far to have been legally condemned are enlisted personnel and junior officers—although those who have spoken out have claimed that they were acting as their superiors ordered. We now know that they had cause to believe so. On December 2, 2002, the secretary of defense gave written authorization for—indeed, issued instructions ordering—the use of procedures banned by the U.S. Army Field Manual as violations of Common Article 3, which is repeated in each of the four Geneva Conventions outlawing torture and cruel treatment. Many people, both American and foreign, now consider that torture is "American." Since it has been practiced at a number of American installations and

* The U.S. Army ran a school for Latin American military officers from 1982 to 1991 using manuals that laid out methods of interrogation and coercion including torture and executions, according to documents released by the Pentagon in September 1996. Some sixty thousand military and police officers, including General Manuel Antonio Noriega, and Julio Roberto Alpirez, who were later prominent in death squads and drug dealing, attended this school. The textbooks were allegedly withdrawn in 1996. But many of the same methods have been inculcated in the personnel that ran the American prisons in Iraq, Cuba, and elsewhere.

required not only a significant amount of equipment (including the jet aircraft that took kidnapped prisoners to torture centers) but also relatively large numbers of American soldiers and intelligence agents—alongside a significant number of foreign (allegedly including Israeli) nationals—it had to be an operation of large scale and adequate funding. Immoral, illegal, and disgusting acts, having been documented by some of the perpetrators (just as many Nazis documented their bestial acts), have now been seen in photographs by hundreds of millions of people throughout the world on television, in newspapers, and on the Internet. The effect on the image of America cannot as yet be documented, but no one believes it to be less than disastrous. Iraqis and other Asians and Africans remark that torture puts America in the league with Saddam Hussein's tyranny. The words "Abu Ghraib," "Guantánamo," "Bagram," and "extraordinary rendition" are now part of America's image in the world community. And the potential damage is not only in foreign relations. As the former general counsel of the U.S. Navy, Alberto J. Mora, who struggled to stop the policy of torture, said to *New Yorker* correspondent Jane Mayer, "If cruelty is no longer declared unlawful, but instead is applied as a matter of policy, it alters the fundamental relationship of man to government. It destroys the whole notion of individual rights. . . . If you make this exception, the whole Constitution crumbles. It's a transformative issue."

Even those who close their eyes to torture now also think of America in images of brutal warfare. The horror of the destruction of Fallujah, Tal Afar, and other Iraqi cities, the deluge of reports of casual killing, rape, and murder have, like torture, become the daily fare of television audiences around the world. All this has so altered the perception of America and Americans as to be palpable. William R. Polk was able to walk the streets of Baghdad just a few days before the 2003 American invasion, talking to shopkeepers, peddlers, policemen, and pedestrians, freely and without fear. Today Americans cannot leave their fortified Green Zone except in convoys of armored cars and tanks with helicopters hovering overhead.

Even private American citizens feel unsafe now, not only in Iraq but throughout much of Asia and Africa and even in parts of Latin America and Europe. For official representatives, it is far worse. When George McGovern was the American ambassador to the UN Food and Agriculture Organization in the years before the Iraq war, he was everywhere received warmly and joyfully. Today our ambassadors hunker down in miniature forts; in fact, the nearly three hundred American government overseas installations have been ringed with concrete blast walls, wire fences, and crash-proof vehicle barriers; electronic sensors and video cameras constantly sweep them; armed guards and attack dogs are on patrol; in some places adjoining properties have been leveled and streets closed. Thus American officials are virtually under siege. Visitors and officials alike see them as cages rather than embassies. And it is not only officials who feel the pinch of hostility magnified by the Iraq war; some American businesses have found that their sales have declined.

Is this picture just impressionistic? Look at what the polls tell us. The Pew Research Center poll of some fifteen thousand people in twenty countries in May 2003 showed a precipitous decline in respect and affection for America. Particularly in the Muslim world, the director of the research center commented, "the bottom has fallen out." But not only there. In Germany, favorable views of

America fell from 61 percent in the summer of 2002 to a low of 25 percent at the time of the U.S. invasion in 2003; in France, from 63 percent to a low of 31 percent; in Spain the low point was 14 percent despite the fact that Spain furnished troops for the occupation. In the fall of 2004 ten of the world's leading newspapers conducted another poll: it showed that despite President Bush's assertion that people hate our freedom, almost everywhere people drew a sharp distinction between Americans and the current administration: even among our staunch allies, the English, only 21 percent said they did not like Americans but over 60 percent disliked the Bush administration, and that number hit 77 percent among men and women under twenty-five. Almost everywhere the same proportions prevailed. In our neighbor Canada, 73 percent of the people like Americans but only 36 percent approved of America's government; in France the numbers were 72 percent versus 25 percent; in Spain 47 percent versus 23 percent; in Japan 74 percent versus 34 percent; in Australia, 72 percent versus 36 percent; in Mexico 51 percent versus 30 percent; and in South Korea, 65 percent versus 28 percent. Reacting to these and other indicators of the decline of our position in the world, the Bush administration's undersecretary of state for public diplomacy Margaret Tutwiler testified before Congress that "it will take us many years of hard, focused work" to climb out of this hole.

The latest poll taken in England shows a further disheartening plunge. The reelection of President Bush for a second term, many speculated, wiped out the distinction that had formerly been drawn between the government and the people.

Two dangers are immediately evident. First, the violence of the insurgency and counterinsurgency is pushing Iraq ever closer toward a vicious ethnic-religious civil war in which both American reputations and lives will be increasingly at risk. Second, outside Iraq, a comparable religious war looms ahead, in which our country wages an American Christian crusade against an Islamic jihad. Such a conflict could be interminable. Some of our most senior military officers believe, as Joseph P. Hoar, a retired general of the U.S. Marine Corps, warned the Senate Armed Services Committee and the Senate Foreign Relations Committee, that "we are looking into the abyss." We have a chance to achieve the security we seek in the "war on terrorism," he said, "only when we convince one billion Muslims that we are, in fact, a just society: that we do support peace, justice, equality for all people, that in fact we really are the city on the hill."

CHAPTER 5

How to Get Out of Iraq

IN PREVIOUS CHAPTERS we have discussed *why* America must get out of Iraq. Here we will lay out a plan to show *how* our exit might be accomplished in such a way as to assuage the damage done both to Iraq and to America.

It is in the interest of the United States that we not leave behind an Iraq filled with people who hate America and will seek to revenge themselves for the war. After more than three years of warfare and occupation, a graceful exit cannot be perfectly accomplished. It is always far easier to get into a bad situation than to get out. There is much bitterness against America in Iraq; too many people have lost children, parents, grandparents, neighbors, and friends in what *they believe* to have been an unjust war and a repressive occupation. Whatever its merits and demerits, the old social order has been disrupted; people who were once neighbors are now fearful of one another. Property has been destroyed or damaged. Life savings have been eaten away by inflation, lack of income, and extraordinary costs. The working population has been dispirited by massive and long-lasting unemployment. Millions of people have been reduced to living without electricity or running water or the safe disposal of sewage. To pull out of the very difficult situation in which both Iraq and America find themselves, costs will have to be paid. But the longer we delay in facing realities, the higher those costs will clearly be. Some already will be high, but managing them is better than continuing to incur more. As long as we "stay the course," we can expect the Iraqi situation to worsen—probably rapidly.

Some measures that have been suggested to cope with identified problems are merely palliative. Such measures are dangerous because they are misleading: they seem to offer solutions whereas in fact they merely justify not finding solutions to the fundamental issues. Other suggested measures may be, in and of themselves, attractive, but separated from a coordinated program, they would likely fail. Only in a coherent strategic "package" of remedies will individual measures be effective. Of those measures that address fundamental issues, some will be financial. Those are the ones to which Americans are more accustomed. As a pragmatic and business-oriented people, we are generally good at organizing such activities. Others are more complex and intangible. Alongside the financial measures, indeed prior to them, must be gestures that are primarily political and moral. The first is acknowledgment of the fundamental right of Iraqis to manage their own lives.

Many Americans believe that the Iraqis have not done a very good job of managing their lives in the past and that arising from the occupation and insurgency, they are unlikely to do better very soon. They are right. The press is full of accounts of the conflicts among them, in which Sunnis and Shiis attack one another and Kurds are intent on achieving the maximum safe distance from the Iraqi state. Some Americans believe that, consequently, we should manage their lives for them and provide them with "security" before giving them a chance to express their own objectives. Some even believe that we must divide Iraq into three parts. Conceivably that may happen, but it is not up to us to effect it, and it almost certainly would work against our—and Iraqi—interests. We also have proclaimed our intent to make Iraqis into Americans—that is to say, to turn Iraqis into "democrats." But in the Iraqi experience democracy has been a hollow concept at best, and the word was often used to camouflage special privilege or tyranny. The ways in which we express our dedication to democracy—promulgation of a constitution and the holding of elections—were tried in Iraq under the sponsorship of the British in the 1920s and 1930s and did not produce in Iraq what we think of as popular control of government or democracy. They are unlikely to do so in the foreseeable future. Iraqis will have to find for themselves a system with which they can live with reasonable peace, security, and freedom. That system will almost certainly not be what we have or what we would wish them to have, but we will not be able to force them to live in ways alien to their culture. Attempting this has been a critical failure in our perception of the "meaning" of our war. The Bush administration said that we were there to make Iraq safe for democracy and that the Iraqis would be grateful to us. On the contrary, Iraqis believe that what we are trying to do is to impose upon them an alien way of life. Thus they have struggled against us not only as foreigners but also as foreigners attacking their culture. The interventionist military policy that the neoconservatives convinced the Bush administration to adopt will not work. It is deeply resented. We will have to accept this fact. President Woodrow Wilson's emphasis on the "self-determination of peoples" was not only a political but also a strategic imperative. Nationalism is still the most powerful force of our times. In one country after another it has defeated every attempt by rich, powerful, dominant powers to overturn and recast the lives of the peoples they conquered. In short, as we have seen in three years of war, there are limits to our power, and we must adjust to that reality.

Underlying the divisive forces of separate nationalism, however, burns the pale flame of unity. We have argued that, while the unity of Iraq is in danger and the danger of disintegration of the country will grow the longer the occupation continues, considerable forces hold the country together. Among them is the recognition of the dangers that a balkanized society would face from neighbors and the terrible dislocations a breakup of the nation-state would undoubtedly cause. We cannot predict whether the Iraqis will ultimately be wise enough to cope with these dangers, and we would be foolish to try to do it for them. Indeed, any such moves would be deeply resented by the Iraqis. The notion that we can grandly adjust the way Iraqis live is one of the delusions that got us into the Iraq quicksand in the first place. To keep trying to manage the very structure of Iraq will not help us get out. However much they may disagree among themselves, the Iraqi people, like the Vietnamese, even in the midst of bitter struggles against us, want what we demand for ourselves: the right to govern their own lives in ways they believe are conducive to purposes of independence. People everywhere, and certainly in Iraq, believe self-determination is a fundamental right. That is a right we would be wise to avoid violating as we climb out of the hole into which we have fallen. As President Wilson said when he attempted to reorder American priorities at the end of the First World

War, "There is only one thing that can bind men together, and that is common devotion to right." This sentiment was echoed just after the invasion in 2003 by the Reverend Konrad Raiser, general secretary of the World Council of Churches, who argued that "right" must be defined within a consensus of world opinion, that is, what Thomas Jefferson called "a decent respect to the opinions of mankind." Only if America respects the fundamental right of people in Iraq to determine their own future can America's reputation in the world community, so grievously harmed by the Iraq war, be reconstituted.

Reconstituting America's good name and standing in the world will require blending political, moral, and financial remedies; only thus can we—and the Iraqis—effect the best possible outcome of a bad and deteriorating situation. Consequently, it is crucial to the security of the United States—and to the health of still-feeble moves toward freedom and democracy in Iraq—that America find means to exit the war in Iraq speedily, intelligently, and in ways that will replenish, or at least not further drain, what Republican Party presidential candidate Wendell Willkie memorably called the "reservoir of good will." That almost universal affection for our country has been America's greatest strength. So, as Jefferson said, "let us hasten to retrace our steps and to regain the road which alone leads to peace, liberty, and safety."

While we will treat separately for the sake of clarity the steps we need to take to progress along Jefferson's "road," we emphasize that they must be considered as elements of a mutually reinforcing agenda. In the following paragraphs we will highlight the major categories of actions that could move Iraq, America, and the world community toward a safer, sounder, and more decent postwar world.

We will also attempt to give both a time framework and some rough approximations of the costs and benefits of each action we propose. We begin with the fundamental requirement: the withdrawal of our troops as well as the small troop contingents from other countries.

■   Staying in Iraq is not an option. Even among Americans who were the most eager to invade Iraq, probably a majority now urge that we find a way out. They include not only civilian strategists and other "hawks" but also senior military commanders and, perhaps most fervently, combat soldiers. Even those Iraqis whom our senior officials regard as the most pro-American are determined that American military personnel leave their country. The most senior living Iraqi official from the prerevolutionary era, former foreign minister Adnan Pachachi, wrote privately to William Polk that "the truth is all Iraqis, without exception, want an early departure of the foreign troops." His observation was backed up by a *USA Today*/CNN/Gallup poll that shows that 81 percent of Iraqis regard Americans not as liberators but as occupiers. This is the reality of the situation in Iraq, and we must acknowledge the Iraqis' right to ask us to leave and set a firm date for withdrawal.

Withdrawal is not only a political imperative but also a strategic requirement. Before the American invasion, Iraq was devoid of terrorists; today, as the American command and senior civil and military officers have repeatedly admitted, Iraq has become the primary recruiting and training ground for them. As Lieutenant General William Odom, the former head of the National Security Agency, put it: "We're achieving Bin Laden's ends." The longer American troops remain in Iraq, the more Iraqis and others will regard America as their enemy and the more recruits will flood into the ranks of those who oppose America not only in Iraq but elsewhere. The first step in the process of stopping the hemorrhaging of American interests is withdrawal of our troops. Since current U.S. expenditures run at approximately $237 million per diem—almost $10 million an hour—and with costs rising nearly 30 percent yearly,* America has a clear financial interest in complying with Iraqi demands for early withdrawal. We suggest that phased withdrawal should begin on or before December 31, 2006, with the promise to make every effort to complete it by June 30, 2007.

Withdrawal is not without financial costs. These costs are unavoidable and will have to be paid sooner or later. The decision to withdraw soon will not require additional expenditures—on the contrary, it will effect massive savings—but it will require careful planning. Let us be absolutely clear: we are not recommending what opponents of withdrawal call "cut and run." What we are proposing will avoid being forced out; rather, American troops will leave in an orderly way, on a reasonable schedule, and in a manner that will prevent further damage to American interests. Those interests include avoiding the harm that could be inflicted on our society if demagogues are given an opportunity to use withdrawal to divide us. We should remember what the Nazis did in Germany—telling their

---

* While its figures do not include all costs, the Congressional Research Service listed direct costs at $77.3 billion in 2004, $87.3 billion in 2005, and $101.8 billion in fiscal year 2006. Even if troop withdrawals begin this year, costs (including Afghanistan) are thought likely to rise by $371 billion during the withdrawal period. See Jonathan Weisman, "Projected Iraq War Costs Soar: Total Spending Is Likely to More Than Double, Analysis Finds," *Washington Post*, April 27, 2006.

people that their army had won World War I but were stabbed in the back by traitorous politicians at home. Some irresponsible French politicians tried the same tactic after their disastrous war in Algeria, and sad to say, some Americans made similar charges at the end of the Vietnam War—that the army had "won" only to be sold out by the politicians. But in both of these cases and in Iraq today, military force did not in fact accomplish the stated goals of the war. In some respects the invasion of Iraq has been more of a failure than our sad and bloody experience in Vietnam. Vice President Cheney continues to oppose withdrawal as he did on CNN on June 22, 2006. He asserted that "absolutely the worst possible thing we could do at this point would be to validate and encourage the terrorists by doing exactly what they want us to do, which is to leave." To the contrary, if they are smart, terrorists want us to stay because we are creating the conditions in which they thrive. A study at the Army War College's Strategic Studies Institute makes clear that the insurgency in Iraq is expanding and *becoming more deadly as a consequence of U.S. policy.* And a task force set up by the libertarian Cato Institute judged that "a long-term military presence in Iraq would be disastrous for the United States." So every effort must be made to effect the withdrawal of American forces rapidly, with the least possible damage both to America and to Iraq.

Let us be clear: withdrawal will cause some damage. But damage is inevitable, no matter if we stay or leave. At the end of every insurgency we have studied, a certain amount of chaos erupted as the participants readjusted their relations with one another and sought to establish a new civic order, each on its own terms. This predictable turmoil gives rise to the argument, still being put forth by some avowed hawks, that Americans must, in President Bush's phrase, "stay the course." It is a false argument. When a driver is on the wrong road and headed for the abyss, "staying the course" is a bad idea. Only lemmings find that argument compelling. A nation afflicted with a failing and costly policy is not well served by those who call for more of the same. It is also naive to think that we can accomplish in the future what we are failing to accomplish in the present. We are as powerless to prevent the turmoil that will happen when we withdraw as we have been to stop the insurgency. But when we withdraw, we will remove a major cause of the insurgency. As Major Brent Lilly, head of a Marine civil affairs team, told a *Washington Post* reporter on August 4, 2006, "Nobody wants us here . . . if we leave, all the attacks would stop, because we'd be gone." Moreover, we can be helpful to the Iraqis—and protect our own interests—by ameliorating the social and economic conditions and smoothing the edges of conflict. The first way we can be helpful is to contribute to a "bridging" effort between the occupation and complete independence.

■   To this end, the Iraqi government would be wise to request the short-term services of an international force to police the country during and immediately after the period of American withdrawal. Such a force should be on only temporary duty, with a firm date fixed in advance for withdrawal. Our estimate is that Iraq would need it for about two years after the American withdrawal is complete. During this period the force probably could be slowly but steadily cut back, both in personnel and in deployment. Its activities would be limited to enhancing public security. Consequently, the armament of this police force should be restricted. It would have no need for tanks or artillery or offensive aircraft but only light equipment. It would not attempt, as have American troops, to battle the insurgents. Indeed, after the withdrawal of American and British regular troops and the roughly 25,000 foreign mercenaries, the insurgency, which was aimed at achieving that objective, would lose public support; without that support and no longer having a legitimate national role, it would lose power. Then gunmen would either put down their weapons or become publicly identified as outlaws. This outcome has been the experience of insurgencies in Algeria, Kenya, Ireland (Eire), and elsewhere.

If the Iraqi government were receptive to this suggestion, it would find such an international "stabilizing" force most acceptable if its composition were drawn from Arab or at least Muslim countries.* Specifically, it should be possible under the aegis of the Arab League or the United Nations to obtain contingents of, say, three thousand men each from Morocco, Algeria, and Egypt. If Jordan and Syria could be led to give up their claims on Iraq, troops from those countries might also join. If additional troops were required, or if any of these governments were deemed unacceptable to Iraq or unwilling to serve, application could be made to such Muslim countries as Pakistan, Malaysia, and/or Indonesia. At the option of the Iraq government, other countries might be included.

It would be to the benefit of both Iraq and the United States for the United States to pay for this force. Assuming that a ballpark figure for the cost of the force is $500 per man per day and that fifteen thousand men would be involved for two years, the overall cost would be roughly $6 billion. That is approximately 2 percent of what the American direct or congressionally appropriated costs (that is, not including the overall costs to American society) would be for a

* As former Bush adviser General Brent Scowcroft suggested in "Focusing on 'Success' in Iraq," *Washington Post*, January 16, 2006.

similar period in continuing the war. The force would thus be a great financial saving to Americans—not to mention that it would avoid further casualties—and it would give Iraq a breathing space to help it recover from the trauma of the occupation in a way that does not violate national sensibilities.

The American subvention should be paid to the Iraqi government, which would then "hire" the services of the forces on a government-to-government basis. Additionally, since the American military now has vast amounts of equipment in Iraq, that part which is suitable (particularly transport, communications, and light arms) could be turned over to this new multinational force rather than being shipped home or destroyed.

■   During the period of withdrawal, if the Iraqi government requests American assistance, America should do all it reasonably can to assist it in embodying and training a permanent national police force comprised of Iraqi citizens to replace the temporary international force. It is in the national interest of Iraq and in the interest of its current—or any conceivable future—government that it provide, as soon as possible, reasonable public security for its citizens. Once American troops are withdrawn, the Iraqi public is unlikely to continue supporting insurgents, so the level of combat is almost certain to fall. This has been the experience in every comparable guerrilla war. But as the insurgency loses its national justification, new dangers will confront Iraq: "warlordism" (as happened in Afghanistan) and other forms of large-scale crime. This breakdown of public order can best be addressed by a combination of a national police force, subject to central government control, and neighborhood, village, and tribal home guards.

■   Creation of an effective national police force in Iraq is proving very difficult. The historical ethnic, religious, and regional political divisions have been exacerbated by the occupation. They are now so bitter that they may preclude a unified organization at least for the time being. For this reason, among others, Iraq needs a cooling-off period with multinational security assistance after the American withdrawal. But the Americans clearly cannot be the one to overcome the doleful legacy of the past: after three years of American efforts, "the police are a battered and dysfunctional force that has helped bring Iraq to the brink of civil war."* Creating a minimally usable national police force is (and must be) an Iraqi national task, in which American interference would be (and has been) counterproductive. The creation and solidification of a national police force will probably require some years, perhaps at a rough estimate four to five, although it would progressively become involved from the beginning of the American evacuation and the installation of the Arab or Muslim peacekeeping force. We suggest that the American withdrawal package should include provision of $1 billion to help the Iraqi government create, train, and equip such a force. This is roughly the cost of four days of the American occupation.

To a considerable extent, the national police force can be—and will be, whether the United States or any Iraqi government likes it or not—supplemented by neighborhood, village, and tribal home guards. Such groups are traditional in Iraqi society. But in the current circumstances they constitute a double-edged sword. Inevitably, they mirror the ethnic, religious, and political communities whom they

* Michael Moss and David Rohde, "Misjudgments Marred U.S. Plans for Iraqi Police," *New York Times*, May 21, 2006.

are to guard and from whom they are drawn. Insofar as they are restricted, each to its own community, and are carefully monitored by a relatively open and benign government, they will enhance security; allowed free rein to move at will outside their home areas, however, they will menace public order. The only means to restrict them are two: the central government police and the leaders of their respective communities. America has no useful role to play in these affairs, as experience has demonstrated.*

■ America should immediately release all prisoners of war it holds and close its detention centers. It has already begun this process, although on a small scale. (See also pages 115 and 116.)

■ It is not in the interest of Iraq to encourage the growth and heavy armament of a reconstituted Iraqi army. The civilian government of Iraq should, and hopefully will, take into account in considering its policy toward the creation of a regular army that previous Iraqi armies have frequently acted against civil governments and Iraqi citizens. Iraqi armies have been a source not of defense but of disruption. Thus, until balancing civic institutions have time and opportunity to grow, the creation of an army is not in Iraq's interest. America cannot prevent the reconstitution of an Iraqi army, but it should not, as it is currently doing, encourage it at an estimated cost of $2.2 billion. Where possible, it should encourage the transfer of

* The head of the American effort during the occupation to negotiate with these groups, Matt Sherman, essentially concludes that there was little Americans could do to control them. "Iraq's Militias: Many Little Armies, One Huge Problem," *International Herald Tribune*, March 9, 2006.

the soldiers it has already recruited to a national police force or to a national reconstruction corps modeled on a modified version of the U.S. Corps of Engineers to undertake the rebuilding of infrastructure damaged by the war.

■   The United States could marginally assist in the creation and training of a national reconstruction corps with an allocation of, say, $500 million, or roughly the cost of two days of the occupation.

■   Withdrawal of American forces must include immediate cession of work on U.S. military bases. Some of the more than one hundred bases have already been turned over, at least formally, to Iraqi government officials or closed. We are told that fourteen "enduring bases" for American troops are now under construction in Iraq. The largest five are already massive, amounting to virtual cities. The Balad Air Base, thirty miles north of Baghdad, has a miniature golf course, two PXs, a Pizza Hut, a Burger King, and a prison. Another, still under construction at Al-Asad, will cover up to twenty square miles. Although Secretary of Defense Rumsfeld stated on December 25, 2005, that "at the moment there are no plans for permanent bases . . . It is a subject that has not even been discussed with the Iraqi government," and although the deputy for planning of the U.S. Central Command, General Mark Kimmitt, said, "We do not intend to have any permanent bases in Iraq," their remarks are belied by actions on the ground. In fact, today the bases are growing in size and are being given aspects of permanency. The most critical are remote military bases. They should be closed. The American base at Baghdad International Airport, ironically named Camp Victory, should be the last military base to be closed, as it will be useful in the process of disengagement. Closing these bases is doubly important: for America, they are expensive and will be redundant; for Iraqis, they symbolize a hated occupation and would prevent any Iraqi government from feeling independent. The Iraqis realize that as long as America retains military bases in Iraq, any Iraqi government will live, literally, under the American gun. That is a lesson they learned from their own recent history. For decades after Great Britain declared Iraq "independent," it maintained remote military installations from which it could dominate or overturn Iraqi governments. Absent an American withdrawal and deactivation of the military bases, the insurgency will almost certainly continue.

■ Americans should withdraw from the Green Zone, their vast, sprawling complex in the center of Baghdad. As mentioned earlier, the United States has spent or is spending $1 billion on its headquarters within the Green Zone, which contains or will contain some three hundred houses, a Marine barracks, and twenty-one other buildings, together with its own electrical, water, and sewage systems. The Green Zone should be turned over to the Iraqi government no later than December 31, 2007.

■ Before the turnover the United States should buy, rent, or build a "normal" embassy for a much-reduced complement of U.S. officials. Symbolically, the embassy should not be in the Green Zone, the seat of the occupational government that is staffed by some two thousand American officers and Iraqi personnel. How much of the $1 billion being spent in the Green Zone can, at this point, be saved is unknown, but assuming that a reasonable part of it can, creating a new American embassy for an appropriate staff of not more than five hundred American officials should present no additional cost. In so far as is now practical, the new building should not be designed as though it were a beleaguered fortress in enemy territory.

Thus from military, political, and cultural considerations, withdrawal is imperative. It is also in America's interest on financial grounds. Ceasing construction and withdrawing from these bases should save American taxpayers many billions of dollars over the coming two years. This is quite apart from the cost of the troops they would house—about $25 billion a year for each division.

■ Mercenaries (euphemistically known as Personal Security Detail) are now provided by a whole new industry of more than fifty "security" firms. Comprising at least 25,000 armed men, they constitute a force larger than the British troop contingent in the "coalition." Although hired either directly or indirectly with U.S. government funds, these men operate outside the control—and outside the jurisdiction of the military justice systems—of the British and American armies and are not subjected to Iraqi justice; they are, literally, the "loose cannons" of the Iraq war. They must be withdrawn rapidly and completely lest they be hunted down and killed, as were the troops created by the British in the 1920s (the "levies"), or lest they further damage American interests. The way to withdraw them is simple: stop the payments we make to them.

■ Much must be done to dig up and destroy land mines and unexploded ordnance and, where possible, to clean up depleted uranium in artillery shells and their targets. These dangerous tasks require professional training, but turning over as much of the work as possible to Iraqi contractors, who would employ Iraqi labor, would help jump-start the economy and would be of immediate and desperately needed benefit to the millions of Iraqis who are now out of work. There is considerable experience with demining from the Balkans, Afghanistan, and elsewhere. Once the extent of the problem is known (the UN Environment Program has already published a preliminary "Assessment of Environmental 'Hot Spots' in Iraq"*), the costs can be estimated. Whatever they are, America should not leave this dangerous waste behind. It should make available to the Iraqi government a fund of approximately $250 million—roughly one day's wartime expenditure—to assist in surveys and planning for the removal. Then, once the extent of the problem is estimated, America should fund a program to eradicate the danger.

These elements of the withdrawal package may be regarded as basic. Without them, Iraqi society will have little chance of recovering or its government of becoming effective. Without them, American interests in the Middle East and indeed throughout the world will be damaged. Compared to the cost of our current operation, they are inexpensive and will effect major savings.

Building on these elements are other actions that could benefit both America and Iraq by helping Iraq create a safe and habitable environment. To these second-tier policies we now turn.

■ Property damage incurred during the invasion and occupation has been estimated at between $100 billion and $200 billion. Rebuilding should be, and can be, done by Iraqis, alleviating the socially

* United Nations Development Program study identified as E.06.III.D.13 ISBN: 9280726501, 166 pages.

crippling rate of unemployment, but the United States will have to make a generous contribution if progress is to be made. Some of its aid should take the form of grants; much could be in the form of loans. The funds should be paid over to the Iraqi government, since increasing the power and public acceptance of that government would be sound policy as America leaves. The Iraqis will probably regard such grants or loans as reparations. Americans may regard this as galling, but it is probably inevitable. Worse, at least some of the money will probably be misspent or siphoned off by cliques within the government. It would be to the benefit of the Iraqi people if some form of oversight could be exercised over the funds, but constituting such a body would tend to undercut the legitimacy and authority of the government, which itself will probably be reconstituted during or shortly after the American withdrawal. Proper use of aid funds has been a perennial problem everywhere; America's own record during the occupation has been reprehensible, with 72 cases involving American contractors, officials, and officers being investigated for criminal charges and generally marred by massive waste, incompetence, and outright dishonesty now being investigated for criminal prosecutions. No fledgling Iraqi government is likely to do better. The best that can be hoped for is that reconstruction funds will be portioned out to village, town, and city councils. Enhancement of such groups will go far toward achieving the avowed American aim of strengthening democracy, as Iraqis in increasing numbers at the "grassroots" take charge of their own affairs.

■   After an inspection tour of Iraq in April and May 2006, during which he met with all the senior American officials, General Barry

R. McCaffrey (Ret.), who is now adjunct professor of international affairs at West Point, concluded, "It would be misguided policy to fail to achieve our political objective after a $400 billion war because we refused to sustain the requirement to build a viable economic state."* We agree.

To reconstruct Iraq in this way, the first task would be to ascertain the full extent of the damage, help to plan local reconstruction efforts, and create the required supervisory organization. Possibly, the organized reconstruction in Britain and Germany at the end of the Second World War could provide a useful guide to how this might be undertaken in Iraq. We suggest that the United States allocate for surveys, planning, and organization the sum of $1 billion (or roughly four days of the wartime expenditure). After such a survey is completed, the American government will have to determine, in consultation with the Iraqi government and presumably with its occupation partner, the British government, what it is willing to pay for reconstruction. We urge that the compensation be generous, as generosity will go far to repair the damage to the American reputation and American strategic interests caused by the war.

Insofar as practical, Iraqi engineers, contractors, tradesmen, and construction workers should be employed in postwar reconstruction. Their involvement will be a point of pride for Iraqis, but it will also help to reduce Iraq's crippling rate of unemployment, which was caused by the war, the embargo, and the insurgency. Iraqi engineers are among the ablest in the Middle East and can carry out important

* Barry R. McCaffrey, "Memorandum for Colonel Mike Meese and Colonel Cindy Jebb of the Department of Social Sciences," United States Military Academy West Point.

work more efficiently and at less cost than engineers brought in under contract from abroad. This fact was demonstrated in the rapid and effective rebuilding of the country after the 1991 Gulf War.

■   Parallel to the reconstruction of damaged buildings and other infrastructure is the demolition of the ugly monuments of warfare. Work should be undertaken to dismantle and dispose of the miles of concrete blast walls and wire barriers erected around American installations. Unlike the building projects, demolition should probably be under central government control, although local authorities will, probably spontaneously, raze nearby relics of the occupation. The total cost is unknown, but the United States could offer two days' cost of the current war effort, or $500 million.

■   Another residue of the war and occupation is the intrusion of military facilities on Iraqi cultural sites. Some American facilities have done enormous—occasionally irreparable—damage. In one of the tragedies of the American occupation, one of these bases was built on top of the Babylon World Heritage archaeological site. When they entered Babylon, American troops "turned the site into a base camp, flattening and compressing tracts of ruins as they built a helicopter pad and fuel stations. The soldiers filled sandbags with archaeological fragments and dug trenches through unexcavated areas, while tanks crushed slabs of original 2,600-year-old paving." As one visitor described what he saw, "It has been ransacked, looted, torn up, paved over, neglected and roughly occupied . . . Signs of military occupation are everywhere—trenches, bullet casings, shiny coils of razor wire and blast walls stamped 'This side Scud protection.' "* Babylon was not the only casualty. The five-thousand-year-old site of Kish is perhaps the next most damaged. The list goes on. Indeed, as the seedbed of civilization, Iraq is itself a virtual museum. It is hard to put a spade into the earth without disturbing a part of the record of the creation of our shared cultural heritage. America should set up a fund of, say, $250 million (one day's cost of the war) to be administered by an ad hoc committee drawn from the Iraqi Museum of Antiquities or its Board of Antiquities, the British Museum, the Smithsonian Institution, the World Monuments Fund, and America's perhaps most prestigious archaeological organization, the Oriental Institute of the University of Chicago, to assist in the restoration of sites its troops have damaged. Americans should not wish to go down in history as yet another barbarian invader of this ancient land long referred to as "the cradle of civilization."

■   Independent accounting of Iraqi funds is urgently required. During the period of the rule of the American-run Coalition Provisional Authority, the UN handed over billions of dollars generated by the sale of Iraq petroleum to the CPA, on the understanding that the monies would be used for the benefit of the Iraqi people and would be accounted for by an independent auditor. The CPA delayed the audit month after month and did not complete it before the CPA

* Jeffrey Gettleman. "Unesco Aims to Put Magic Back in Babylon," *New York Times,* April 14, 2006, and Rupert Cornwell, "US colonel offers Iraq an apology of sorts for devastation of Babylon," *Independent,* April 15, 2006. Iraq has some ten thousand significant archaeological sites. A coordinated effort under the German Archaeological Institute is attempting to work out means to repair as much of the damage as possible.

ceased to exist. An independent audit should be immediately undertaken by a reputable international firm. The fee for such an activity is
likely to run as high as $100 million, which the United States is
morally obligated to provide.* If U.S. officials misused or misappro-
priated funds, the monies should be repaid to the proper Iraqi authority. This amount, if any, cannot now be predicted.

While the fund that the UN turned over to the CPA is the
largest amount in dispute, it is not the only case of possible misap-
propriation. Among several others that have been reported, perhaps
the most damaging to Iraq is a project allocated to Halliburton's subsidiary Kellogg, Brown and Root (KBR) as a part of the $2.4 billion
no-bid contract awarded to Halliburton in 2003. The now-failed
$75.7 million project was supposed to repair the junction of some fif-
teen oil pipelines linking the oil fields with terminals. Despite engineering studies indicating that as conceived the project was likely to
fail, KBR went ahead and allegedly withheld reports from the Iraqi
Oil Ministry on the failure until it had used up all the money. As
Griff Witte reported in the *Washington Post* on July 12, 2006, "Government audits turned up more than $1 billion in questionable costs"
by KBR's parent company, Halliburton. During 2005, the U.S. Army
paid the company or its subsidiaries more than $7 billion and is ex-
pected to pay out $4–$5 billion in 2006. America should make every
effort to leave Iraq with clean hands.

---

* Estimates were given to us by Charles Harris, chairman of Harris and
Harris, George Polk, president of The Cloud, and others based in part on the
cost of the audit of the fall of the Enron Corporation. They have pointed out
that private firms may be reluctant to take on such a difficult and politically
unpopular task. If so, some special agency of the United Nations or even the
U.S. Congress may be the court of last resort.

■ The United States should make reparations to Iraqi civilians for loss of lives and property it caused. The British have already begun to do so in their zone. The policy of the Ministry of Defence "has, from the outset of operations in Iraq, been to recognize the duty to provide compensation to Iraqis where this is required by the law [and . . .] between 1 June 2003 and 30 November 2005, 2019 claims have been registered."* American compensation for noncombatant casualties appears to be more haphazard than the British, but individual military units are authorized to make "condolence payments" of up to $2,500. This amount compares to $400,000 paid to the beneficiaries of an American military casualty.†

While no precise legal precedent (from the Korean or other wars) points to the requirement for American compensation for noncombatant casualties, the U.S. Congress in April 2003 passed The Iraq War Supplemental Appropriations Act. The act avoided the word "compensation," but assumed the obligation to pay "assistance for families of innocent Iraqi civilians who suffer losses as a result of military operations." We believe that it would be to the interest of America to act generously to do what is now possible to compensate the victims or their heirs. This would be a continuation of the Marshall Plan and other aid programs that so powerfully redounded to America's interest after World War II. The following suggests orders of magnitude that could be considered.

The number of civilians killed or wounded during the invasion

---

* Martin Hemming (British Ministry of Defence), private communication to William R. Polk, May 18, 2006.

† Andrew J. Bacevich, "What's an Iraqi Life Worth?" *Washington Post,* July 9, 2006.

and occupation, particularly in such sieges as those of Fallujah, Tal Afar, and Najaf, is unknown. Estimates run from 30,000 to well over 100,000 killed and an unknown number seriously wounded or incapacitated. Assuming the number of unjustified deaths at 50,000 and the compensation per person at $10,000, the probable total allocation would be approximately $500 million. The number incapacitated is unknown, but the best guess we have been able to make is between 15,000 and 25,000. Assuming 20,000 and taking the same figure as death benefits, the total cost would be $200 million. Possible compensation for deaths and grievous wounds would thus add up to the cost of about three days of the American occupation of Iraq.

While complete restitution can never be made for lives lost or bodies damaged, the United States should make every effort—and act in such a way that its good intent is patent—to make amends for the inadvertent pain it caused these people. The dominant voice in the decisions affecting this effort must be Iraqi, but in supplying the funds, the United States can reasonably insist on the creation of some quasi-independent body, composed of both Iraqis and respected foreigners, operating under the umbrella of an internationally recognized organization such as the International Federation of Red Cross and Red Crescent Societies, and/or the World Health Organization to assess and distribute compensation.*

■   To assist in the growth of civic institutions, America should offer not directly but through suitable international, multinational, or nongovernmental organizations a number of financial induce-

* We are grateful to Henry Steiner, founder of the Human Rights Program of the Harvard Law School, for his advice on this matter.

ments and supports. These should include fellowships for the training of lawyers, judges, journalists, and a variety of nongovernmental social workers and other civil affairs workers at Iraqi, European, Asian, or American educational institutions. We have numerous precedents for such action, including the Fulbright fellowships and training programs of the Salzburg Seminar and other institutions. While this effort will take study and planning, the United States could agree to create a fund of, say, two days' cost of the war, or $500 million, to promote it.

■ Assistance to grassroots organizations and professional societies could help to encourage the return to Iraq of the thousands of skilled men and women who left the country in the years following the 1991 Gulf War. Perhaps some form of relocation allowance and supplementary pay could be administered by, for example, the Iraqi engineers' union. Medical practitioners could similarly receive grants through the Iraqi medical association. Exiled or émigré university professors might thus be courted by Iraqi universities drawing on such funds. Similarly, teachers would be assisted by the teachers' union and/or the Ministry of Education. Assuming the total personnel in these categories aggregates to 10,000, let us assume an average of $50,000 each or a total of $500 million. Roughly two days' cost of the war would be a very small price to pay for a program that would contribute greatly to the health and vigor of Iraqi society and to the repairing of America's image.

■ The Iraqi government has already indicted a number of members of the former regime. While they are now physically in American custody, their legal status is no longer under American control. They should be turned over to the Iraqi authorities. The status of other, so-far-unindicted prisoners now being held by the Americans will have to be determined. Presumably the Iraqi government will assert its authority to do so; consequently, such records as the American authorities have should be turned over to the Iraqi Ministry of Justice and/or the courts. But since the number of prisoners is very large (perhaps 14,000 to 16,000), every effort should be made to expedite their release. Perhaps the easiest method would be to release immediately all prisoners accused of "political" offenses—that is, involvement in the insurgency. A separate category of prisoners, those accused of actual criminal acts (rape, robbery, or smuggling, for example) should be turned over to the Iraqi authorities. What to do with men and women from other countries who took part in the Iraqi insurgency is more complex. In no case should they be turned over to countries where there is reason to believe they will be tortured or executed; perhaps some form of exile in a safe haven, for which there is ample precedent, can be arranged under the auspices of the International Committee of the Red Cross in collaboration with the Red Crescent.*

Meanwhile a respected nongovernmental organization should be appointed to process claims of and pay compensation to those who have been tortured, as defined by the Common Article 3 of the

---

* America would do well to avoid acting in any way comparable to the shameful action of the Vichy French government in turning over soldiers who had fought in the Spanish Civil War to the Nazis, who executed them, and its own shameful action at the end of the Second World War in turning over to the Soviet Union Cossacks, other Russians, and members of minorities, most of whom also were summarily executed.

four Geneva Conventions (as stipulated by Directive 23-10 and the
U.S. Army Field Manual 27-10 on the Law of Land Warfare) or
who have suffered long-term imprisonment. Amnesty International's latest study* suggests that about 3,800 people have been held
for over a year and more than two hundred for two years or more
without charge. This action constitutes a clear violation of the long-
treasured American right to habeas corpus and probably is also a violation of the Geneva Conventions, to which America is a party. The
number subjected to torture is unknown, but it is presumed to include a large portion of those incarcerated. We have not been able to
estimate the cost of a program of compensation or even to find a legal
agreement on the basis on which it could be estimated. Given that
this is legally uncharted territory, it should perhaps be approached
not legally but politically and morally to find the measure of justifi-
able compensation. The very act of *assessing* damages would itself, we
suggest, be a part of the healing process.†

■   The United States should not object to the Iraqi government
voiding all oil contracts for petroleum exploration, development, and
marketing made during the American occupation, so that these can
be renegotiated or thrown open to fair bidding. The Iraqi government
and public believe that because Iraqi oil has been sold at a discount to
American companies and because long-term "production sharing
agreements" are highly advantageous to concessionaires, they are unfair. Indeed, the form of concession set by the CPA, as mentioned earlier, has been estimated to cost Iraq over the terms of the contracts

* *Beyond Abu Ghraib: Detention and Torture in Iraq,* March 6, 2006.
† Perhaps somewhat along the lines of the South African Truth Commission.

upward of $200 billion in lost revenues. Since most Iraqis, and indeed many foreigners, believe that America invaded Iraq to take its lightweight and inexpensively produced oil, it is in the long-term interest of both Iraq and the United States that all dealings in oil be fair and be seen to be fair. Only on this condition can the industry be reconstituted and enabled to make a major contribution to Iraqi well-being and to world energy needs. Once the attempt to create American-controlled monopolies or unfair contracts is abandoned, investment could take place in a rapid and orderly manner. So we anticipate no cost to the American government connected to this reform.

■   The United States should encourage with large-scale assistance various UN agencies—including the World Health Organization, UNICEF, The World Food Program and the Food and Agriculture Organization—as well as nongovernmental organizations to help reconstitute the Iraqi public health system through the rebuilding of hospitals and clinics and the purchase of diagnostic and therapeutic equipment. One reason for turning to respected international organizations to supervise this program is that when the CPA undertook it, the funds were apparently squandered. In this effort, one American company, Parsons, has been investigated for having taken what was described as a "generous cost-plus" contract to rebuild 142 clinics at a cost of over $200 million; while it spent all the money, it built only twenty clinics.

A detailed study prepared for the United Nations Millennium Development Goals (UNMDG) project gives estimates that could serve as a guide for constructing and equipping new health centers, rural hospitals, and main hospitals and upgrading or repairing those damaged. The UNMDG figures throw into sharp relief the disappointing results of the American program. The UN study did not focus on Iraq but provides guidelines for other countries with similar characteristics. Based on population size, the numbers might be on the order of roughly 800 health centers, 150 rural hospitals, and 22 main hospitals. If we assume that three-quarters of these already exist in Iraq, the overall cost for repair of war damage and attrition can be estimated at $43 million. Given the number of people wounded or made ill by the invasion and occupation, Iraq will also need something like two hundred new health centers, forty rural hospitals, and six main hospitals. Building and equipping them might require approximately $130 million. These figures are far lower than estimates we have received for comparable facilities in America.* Assuming that they are low and adding 25 percent to the estimated cost, the total required for physical plants and equipment might be on the order of $220 million. That is somewhat less than one day's cost of the occupation.

Estimating the cost of staffing these installations is complicated because Iraq, at least theoretically, has a highly professional, well-trained, and large corps of health workers at all levels; but many, probably most, of them left the country in the years since the 1991 war. The Iraqi Medical Association has estimated that about three

* Dr. Gary Fleisher, chief of medicine at Children's Hospital of Harvard University, kindly supplied us with estimates for clinics at $250,000 an exam room, plain radiography at $100,000, ultrasonography $50,000, CT scanning $1 million, and a limited laboratory roughly $100,000. He also estimated the cost of medical subspecialists at $55,000 to $100,000 yearly. Dr. Musa Mlanga of the Pasteur Institute supplemented these figures with estimates of his own and the UNMDG study noted above. Drs. Ann Barnet of Children's National Medical Center, David Nathan of the Harvard Medical School, and Phillip Bauman of Roosevelt Hospital also offered helpful suggestions.

thousand registered doctors left Iraq in 2004 alone. Hopefully but not assuredly, they will return to Iraq once the insurgency has ended. Even if they do so, however, younger replacements for them will have to be trained. The UNMDG study suggested that the training period for specialists is about eight years, for general practitioners five years, and for various technicians and support personnel three years. We suggest that such a training program for a select number—say, one hundred general practitioners and perhaps fifty advanced specialists—might be carried out under the auspices of the WHO or perhaps a nongovernmental, international organization such as Médecins Sans Frontières (Doctors Without Borders), since some of this training, at least initially, will have to be done in Europe or America; training for technicians and nurses can be done in Iraq. The costs of this overall health program might be set at $500 million for the first year, when presumably most of the buildings and equipment must be paid for, $400 million for the second, $300 million for the third, $200 million for the fourth, and $100 million for the final year of the program. It is sobering to think that the total cost of rebuilding the public health system of Iraq amounts to less than the cost of eight days of occupation, about $1.7 billion. While the United States has no legal obligation to undertake this task, we believe that it would be of enormous benefit to America over the long run, not only in Iraq but throughout the world.

■   Finally, America should express its condolences for the large number of Iraqis killed, incapacitated, incarcerated, and/or tortured. This gesture may seem difficult to many Americans. We are willing to do a great deal to help other people, but we do not like to seem to offer atonement. Perhaps doing so does not seem "macho" or will strike some Americans as a slur on patriotism. Alien to Americans is the idea of making amends for our actions: we do not like ever to admit that we have been wrong. We also generally believe that whatever the mistakes of the war and occupation, we have done Iraqis a major service by ridding the country of the dictatorship of Saddam Hussein. We have, but in the process we did much damage and disrupted, irreparably damaged, or ended many people's lives. We did much of this inadvertently but some, according to military experts, was unnecessary. A simple gesture of conciliation would go far to shift our relationship from occupation to friendship. It is a gesture without cost but of immense value. Failing to recognize the pain the Iraqi people have suffered could, and we believe would, leave a festering wound.* Making this gesture need not be in any way humiliating to America; it need not do more than express sorrow over the deaths of Iraqi civilians; nor need it involve the payment of any money. But the simple gesture would do more to assuage the sense of hurt in Iraq than all of the above actions.

In summary, the monetary cost of the basic program outlined above might total roughly $7.75 billion. The "second tier" programs cannot be accurately forecast, but the planning and some implementation is likely to cost about $5.5 billion. Assuming that these programs save America two years of occupation, they would offset

* We can judge that it would leave such a wound by observing relations between other countries. Take two very "practical," hard-headed nations, China and Japan. One reason that relations between them continue to be sour, despite the obvious benefits they could derive from close and friendly cooperation, trade, and mutual security, is Japan's refusal to apologize for damage its invasion of China did nearly a century ago. That very old wound shapes their relationship to this day.

expenditures of at least $350 billion and more likely $400–$500 billion. Much more important but of incalculable value are the savings to be measured in what otherwise are likely to be large numbers of shattered bodies and lost lives. Even if our estimates are unduly optimistic and the actual costs turn out to be far higher, we believe that implementing our plan for withdrawal would be perhaps the best investment ever made by our country.

As Americans, we conclude this chapter with a recommendation that carries our deep personal convictions. The nation owes a debt of comprehensive benefits to the young men and women called to military service in Iraq. Americans, including George McGovern, a combat bomber pilot who served in World War II, were given such benefits. They also had the advantage of fighting in a war that had the full support of the American people, who understood that this war was essential to save our civilization from the ravages of Hitler and his aggressive allies. Veterans came home as victorious heroes to a grateful, unified nation. But today the American people and our soldiers increasingly know that the invasion and occupation of Iraq was a mistake ordered by our current Washington leadership. Now is the time for healing the wounds of war and trying to understand its lessons. The veterans of the war in Iraq especially need and deserve a comprehensive rehabilitation—physically, mentally, educationally, and economically, including the highly successful offerings of the World War II G.I. Bill of Rights.

Perhaps Lincoln put it best in his second inaugural address as the bloody Civil War ground to a close, when he called upon all parties to that conflict "to bind up the nation's wounds" and "to care for him who shall have borne the battle."

CHAPTER 6

What Happens If We
Do Not Get Out of Iraq?

IF THE UNITED STATES does not withdraw from Iraq, the war will continue. That means body bags and broken soldiers will continue to flow back to America; large numbers of Iraqi men, women, and children will be wounded or killed; larger numbers of lives of both Iraqis and Americans will be shattered; even more property will be destroyed; and vast funds will be spent that would have made lives safer, more decent, and more rewarding in Iraq, in America, and elsewhere.

Is the cost of staying the course worth it? Military men as well as seasoned diplomats and intelligence officers do not believe the United States has any hope of achieving what President Bush keeps calling "victory." As Lieutenant General William Odom, the former director of the National Security Agency, puts it, "No Iraqi leader with enough power and legitimacy to control the country will be pro-American." Thus failure to withdraw in an orderly fashion, and soon, carries the certainty of eventual withdrawal and the probability that it will be under pressure and in haste.

Done in this fashion, what critics characterize as a "cut and run" withdrawal would cause America to suffer an apparent defeat. Just as this sort of "defeat" has been put to nefarious use by political demagogues in the past both in America and elsewhere, it will likely poison American politics further. More important, it would leave behind an angry, dispirited Iraqi society and a vengeful, empowered mass of recruits for terrorist actions against the United States, both in Iraq and throughout the world.

In desperation, Iraqis and others may engage, on an even larger scale, in such tactics as suicide bombings, which may increase the rate of American wounded and killed. As we have seen in Fallujah and Tal Afar, the impact upon Iraqi civilians would also likely increase so that—already a wounded society—Iraq would virtually disintegrate. Three years of American occupation have greatly inflamed the already delicate relationship among the components of Iraqi society, whereas what Iraq needed was a period of healing. In growing fear, the Sunnis and Shiis, the Arabs and the Kurds, will seek to protect themselves with guns and bombs. They will also take over the fledgling units of police and army and transform them, as indeed both the Kurds and Shiis have begun to do, into mutually hostile militias.

The likely result will be greatly increased regional insecurity. It perhaps will not be immediately evident, but over the next decade the insecurity will create conditions in which warfare is likely, not only within and among the major ethnic and religious sections of Iraqi society but also with neighboring countries. Even short of this development, massive and often forced movements of population within Iraq, with resultant misery and bitterness, are almost certain, and foreign interventions likely. These effects will have unpredictable but pernicious consequences.

■ ■ ■

The costs to American forces are also almost certain to increase. Under pressure and taking casualties, American and British military commanders and operational planners will be unable to resist trying to cut casualties, as in Fallujah and Tal Afar, by application of what Brigadier Nigel Aylwin-Foster,* in an article in the U.S. Army magazine *Military Review,* termed "brute force." In the most likely scenario, American forces would pull back into the vast new bases, from which they will deploy air power. Raining down bombs on Iraqi villages and cities, no matter how "surgical" the strikes or how accurate the intelligence that guides them, will cause America to be seen as a callous, inhumane, and destructive bully. Application of air power will also prove to be a virtual machine to create reactive forces that will produce further chaos and make Iraq ungovernable. To the degree that air power is supplemented by ground attacks—search-and-destroy missions—the results will be even more productive of hopelessness, bitterness, and destructiveness. As this resort to force proves insufficient or ineffective, America is likely to be drawn, as Israel and South Africa have been, into "cantonization." That is, in the quest for security it will create zones, cut off from one another by barriers or by interdicted areas that it cannot control. Such a system of apartheid has not worked elsewhere but has been devastating of the occupied people and damaging to the reputation of the occupier. Ac-

* Deputy commander of the Office of Security Transition in the Coalition Office for Training and Organizing Iraq's Armed Forces. The article was published in November–December 2005; it was strongly endorsed by the second-ranking officer in Iraq, U.S. Lieutenant General Peter Chiarelli.

tions growing out of such a posture will affect one another in a vicious circle leading us ever downward, toward a militaristic state, hated and feared throughout the world.

Some of those who reluctantly agree to withdrawal from Iraq do so because they believe that withdrawal will enable America to engage more successfully in the "long war" against "the universal enemy," terrorism. Is this sensible or not? We urge that, having been lured into a war with Iraq by scare tactics, Americans not give substance to the old saying about jumping from the frying pan into the fire. Let us first consider how real the danger is. As William Pfaff pointed out in the February 12, 2006, issue of *The International Herald Tribune,* the terrorist threat to America has not so far been catastrophic or even serious. "Even if you include the 9/11 casualties, the number of Americans killed by international terrorists since the late 1960s (which is when the State Department began counting them) is about the same as that killed by lightning—or by accident-causing deer, or by severe allergic reactions to peanuts."

But let us assume that the Bush administration is right: that terrorism is a mortal danger to America. Then staying in Iraq and killing Iraqis is the best environment for recruitment the terrorists could have asked for. That is, with one possible exception: the designation of America's enemies in racial or religious terms—as Arabs or Muslims—which would greatly expand their numbers and locations. Then truly the "long war" against "the universal adversary" will be upon us, our children, and our grandchildren. That war will be unwinnable and probably unstoppable, but it will almost certainly destroy the values that we and our ancestors have struggled to achieve and the "good life" to which we all aspire. George Orwell was unduly pessimistic: his bleak vision of the future did not happen as fast as he thought it might—that is, in 1984—but it could well happen in our lifetime.

Getting out of Iraq is the first and most urgent step in avoiding the treacherous, downward spiral toward such a hideous future. Getting out with dignity and making every effort to do so in a way that will leave behind us the best possible climate for rebuilding, regrowth, and peace, as we have set forth in Chapter 5, is the right thing to do. Absent a reversal of American policies, which must begin with a rapid withdrawal from Iraq, the America we have inherited from our Founding Fathers will continue to be in grave, perhaps even mortal, danger.

AFTERWORD

The Lessons of Iraq

ARE THERE ANY LESSONS to be learned from the American venture in Iraq? The great German philosopher of history Georg Wilhelm Friedrich Hegel doubted our capacity to find out. "Peoples and governments," he wrote, "never have learned anything from history or acted on principles deduced from it." Writing about the Vietnam War, the neoconservative American political scientist Samuel P. Huntington suggested that policy-makers would do best to "simply blot out of their mind any recollection of this one." They did. So in at least some ways, the Iraq war has been proof of George Santayana's admonition that, having not learned from history, we were doomed to repeat it. We have repeated some of the worst mistakes of Vietnam in Iraq. The urgent question today is, will the Iraq war itself be similarly blotted out and repeated? The odds are with Hegel and Santayana.

Huntington's argument was based on the notion that the Vietnam War was unique since, as he saw it, imperialism and colonialism have "just about disappeared from world politics." That is, they were fading memories of a now-irrelevant past. But are they? Foreign domination *has* faded from the memories of those of us who live in the wealthy north of the world, but foreign domination is more recent in much of Asia and Africa. There it has not faded from memory. As we have seen, Iraq became "independent" by treaty with Britain in 1922, then by recognition of the League of Nations in 1932. But few Iraqis believe that their country became really independent by either of these acts. Britain controlled the economy and maintained its military presence while it continued to rule Iraq behind a facade of governments it had appointed. It then reoccupied the country during World War II. After the war it ruled through a proxy until he was overthrown in 1958. So was 1958 the date of independence? On the surface yes, but below the surface American and British intelligence manipulated internal forces and governments of neighboring states to influence or dominate successive Iraqi governments. Always the possibility of "regime change" through assassination, a coup d'état, or an invasion was the final trump card in the foreigner's hand.

So worried was Saddam Hussein about American action that, before he decided to invade Kuwait in 1990, he called in the U.S. ambassador to ask, in effect, if the invasion would be okay with Washington. Only when he got what he believed was a "green light" did he act. Either we misled him or he miscalculated. We then invaded, destroyed much of his army and the Iraqi economy, and enforced a regime of severe sanctions that virtually crippled the country. Finally in 2003 we invaded again and imposed upon Iraq a government of our choice. Whatever the justifications for any or all of these actions may have been, they do not add up to independence. So even Iraqis who hated and feared Saddam always felt that they were living under a form of Western control. The simple fact is that the "memories" had not faded, because they were based on current reality.

As Americans have tried to Americanize Iraq, we have often been baffled. Why did the Iraqis not greet our troops with flowers in their hands and smiles on their faces as our government told us they would? Why did only about two Iraqis in every ten regard us as liberators? Why did the man who our senior official said was the most distinguished elder statesman of the country, the prerevolutionary foreign minister, Adnan Pachachi, say, "The truth is that all Iraqis, without exception, want an early departure of the foreign troops"? Why did the Iraqis not thank us for getting rid of Saddam Hussein instead of shooting at us?

As we have pointed out, a part of the answer is that Iraqis believe that we are trying to destroy and then recast their culture and social organization into something alien to them but compatible to us. We have tried this before with little success. A study by Minxin Pei and Sara Kasper for the Carnegie Endowment for International Peace warned us of this fact even before we began implementing our occupation policy.*

We did it anyway, as urged by the neoconservatives, because, according to Samuel Huntington, "we just didn't realize how totally different the culture is in Middle Eastern countries." Differences

---

* Pei and Kasper examined two hundred instances where American military power was projected abroad. Among these were sixteen aimed at "nation building," that is, converting the natives to "the American way." Eleven of the sixteen were outright failures and only two, in tiny and nearby societies, were unambiguous successes. With this record, how, John Tierney asked in the May 17, 2004, *International Herald Tribune*, could so many conservatives "who normally do not trust their government to run a public school down the street, come to believe that federal bureaucrats could transform an entire nation in the alien culture of the Middle East?"

certainly are important, but so are similarities. Other countries, north and south, rich and poor, Christian, Muslim, Buddhist, Hindu, and Jewish, have united against foreign intrusion, even when many hated their own government. The Russians did not use the German attack to try to overthrow Stalin; the Germans fought loyally for Hitler until they were overwhelmed; and the Cubans did not rise against Castro at the Bay of Pigs. No people welcomes a foreign invasion. At least in this way, all peoples are remarkably similar. Thomas Carlyle warned that an emphasis on difference, particularly when it is combined with a sense of superiority (what he called "Orthodoxy or My-doxy and Heterodoxy or Thy-doxy"), can be as misleading as ignorance. But the dissimilar perspectives of power and powerlessness *do* yield very different landscapes. Certainly most Americans had (and many still have) no appreciation for the way Iraqis (and other Asians and Africans), with their material weakness so overbalanced by our military power, see their relationship with us. President Bush saw this imbalance clearly when he remarked that the Iraqis were "not happy they're occupied. I wouldn't be happy if I were occupied either."

Our ignorance of how Iraqis perceived their relationship with us has caused us, often inadvertently, to take actions that many or perhaps most Iraqis have read as imperialist even when, to us, they seemed generous, far-sighted, and constructive. Our basic aim has been to achieve "security." We have repeatedly told the Iraqis that we will get out when their country is secure, but not before. As President Bush put it, "We're not going to leave. We're going to do the job . . . A free Iraq in the midst of the Middle East is vital to future peace and security." Iraqis—and many of our own strategists—point out that what President Bush meant by a "free Iraq" is unlikely to arise in the foreseeable future. So when President Bush says, "We're going to do the job," Iraqis hear him more clearly saying, "We're not going to leave." Is this a reasonable interpretation of our policy? A close reading of the history of insurgencies throughout the world suggests that it is. The sequence we have proclaimed—security before sovereignty—rarely happens; the reverse—sovereignty before security—is the rule. The reason is that when foreigners stay, the native nationalists keep struggling until the foreigners leave, no matter how massive the force used against them or how costly in blood and treasure the fighting is. But when the foreigners get out, the bulk of the population no longer supports the combatants. As Mao Zedong would have put it, the "sea" dries up and the "fish" lose their support. This order of events—sovereignty before security and not the reverse—surely is the lesson of Ireland, Chechnya, Algeria, Vietnam, and even our own revolution. We predict it will be the lesson of Iraq too.

Believing that security comes first has also led our government to concentrate in Iraq on rebuilding an Iraqi army, since such an army appears to offer security at a bargain price. But Iraqis remember the terrible costs to their society of the similar British policy. The army that the British created subverted or overthrew civil governments time after time. A new army, absent balancing civic institutions that can grow only slowly and by internal developments rather than by our fiat, will surely pave the way for another dictatorship.

Our emphasis on security has also encouraged us to think about new Vietnams and new Iraqs. Planning on possible campaigns is under way in Washington, and the construction of scores of bases in Africa, the Middle East, and Central Asia from which to launch new campaigns is already well advanced. Governments in these areas draw the inference that they live at the sufferance of the United States. Naturally, when they can, they seek ways to avoid our often repeated threats of "regime change." Reading the recent history of Iraq, they draw the lesson that Saddam Hussein's fundamental mistake was believing that Iraq could defend itself; it could not, nor can most other states. Many also draw the lesson, which is reinforced by a reading of the U.S. National Security Policy, that we are not the beacon of hope but the knell of doom. In this document we have asserted our "right" to attack any state we believe could rival us, even in its own neighborhood. Only those who believe they can deter us feel secure: that is, those that have the ultimate weapon, the atomic bomb. We have felt the same imperative vis-à-vis the Soviet Union; one after another Britain, France, Israel, China, India, and Pakistan have followed our lead. Acquisition of even a few nuclear weapons provides "security" because the cost of attacking a power armed with them is too high. North Korea today is acting on this assessment. The lesson the North Koreans and probably the Iranians draw from Iraq is that, to be secure *from America,* they must acquire nuclear weapons. A future Iraqi government may come to the same conclusion; almost certainly others will.

Drawing that lesson is, of course, the worst thing that could come out of the Iraq misadventure. Nuclear weapons anywhere are a danger to people everywhere. The only alternative to this ruinously costly drift in international affairs is mutual restraint, which can be achieved only by mutual nuclear disarmament, but current American policies are rushing us, and the world, in exactly the opposite direction. Real security cannot be achieved in an atmosphere of fear by threats or even by preemptive strikes. As the great English statesman Edmund Burke wrote at the time of the American Revolution, "The use of force alone is but temporary. It may subdue for a moment; but it does not remove the necessity of subduing again."

Finally, all war is unpredictable and horrible. Our wise old statesman Benjamin Franklin once said, "There never was a good war." But among wars, guerrilla wars are the worst; at best they are unwinnable, lasting as in Ireland for centuries and in Algeria for a century and a half. Chechens suffered massacre, deportation, rape, and massive destruction at the hands of the Russians for nearly four centuries, and now incorporated into Russia, Chechnya still is not "pacified." Aware of this history, the American neoconservative advisers to our government plan for (and indeed advocate) perpetual war. If they get their wish, then the final lesson of Iraq will emerge from the "fog of war." It is that insurgency and counterinsurgency brutalize whole societies, even those of the victors. This was true of the British in Kenya, French in Algeria, Americans in the Philippines, Russians in Chechnya, and Chinese in Tibet. Hegel may be right—we may not learn; but certainly, we would be wise to heed the warning of Santayana not to "blot" the lessons of this costly adventure out of our minds. It has been our most expensive school.

INDEX

ABOUT THE AUTHORS

GEORGE MCGOVERN, the Democratic Party's nominee for president in 1972, served in the House of Representatives from 1957 to 1961 and in the Senate for eighteen years. He was the president of the Middle East Policy Council in Washington, D.C., for six years and then served as ambassador to the UN Agencies on Food and Agriculture in Rome under President Clinton. He holds the Distinguished Flying Cross for service as a bomber pilot in World War II and the Presidential Medal of Freedom for humanitarian service. A former professor of history, he holds a Ph.D. from Northwestern University. Since leaving the Senate in 1981, he has been a visiting professor at fifteen American and European universities. A heavy speaking schedule has taken him to nearly two thousand college campuses in America, Europe, Asia, Latin America, Canada, Israel, Egypt, Lebanon, and Saudi Arabia. He is the author of a dozen books and numerous articles in major journals and newspapers.

WILLIAM R. POLK studied at Harvard and Oxford and taught at Harvard until he was appointed to be the member of the State Department's Policy Planning Council responsible for the Middle East in 1961. He served as head of the interdepartmental task force on the Algerian war and was a member of the crisis management subcommittee during the Cuban Missile Crisis. In 1965, he became professor of history at the University of Chicago and founded its Middle East Studies Center. In 1967, he became president of the Adlai Stevenson Institute of International Affairs. At the request of Israeli Prime Minister Golda Meir, he negotiated a cease-fire between Israel and Egypt in 1970. Author of a number of books on history, international relations, and the Middle East, including, most recently, *Understanding Iraq*, he is now working on a book on insurgency, guerrilla warfare, and terrorism.